The authors

The authors formed the Directorate of one of the HEFCE-funded Centres for Excellence in Teaching and Learning: ASKe (Assessment Standards Knowledge exchange) based at Oxford Brookes University. ASKe has now been incorporated into the Faculty of Business Pedagogy Research Centre.

All the principal authors work at Oxford Brookes University.

Professor Margaret Price is Director, Faculty of Business Pedagogy Research Centre.

Professor Chris Rust is Associate Dean (Academic Policy).

Berry O'Donovan is Academic Lead in the Department of Business and Management and a Principal Lecturer for Student Experience.

Dr Karen Handley is Reader in the Department of Business and Management.

Dr Rebecca Bryant was the ASKe Centre Manager and now combines working as a university project manager with running her own freelance writing and editorial business.

List of figures

Figure 2.1	*Approaches to developing student understanding of assessment standards*	*25*
Figure 2.2	*A limited example of an assessment grid*	*30*
Figure 2.3	*The student cycle*	*40*
Figure 2.4	*The staff cycle*	*40*
Figure 2.5	*The cultivated community of practice model*	*41*
Figure 3.1	*Stobart's one-handed clock*	*51*
Figure 3.2	*The buttressed building model in relation to automotive engineering*	*58*
Figure 6.1	*Student experiences and responses to assessment feedback*	*123*
Figure 6.2	*The temporal dimension of student engagement with assessment feedback*	*124*

Contents

Preface   1

Acknowledgements   5

1   Introduction: Focus, Aims and Structure   7

2   A Theoretical Perspective: a Matrix and a
    Cultivated Community of Practice Model   23

3   Planning Assessment   45

4   Pre-Assessment Activity   63

5   Assessment Activity   85

6   Post-Assessment Activity: Feedback   105

7   Community   131

8   Conclusion   147

    Bibliography   153

    Index   165

    Glossary   169

Preface

Higher education and the environment in which it operates has undergone dramatic changes since the first moves to increase participation rates, broaden the curriculum and diversify programmes were made in the second half of the twentieth century. The importance of assessment and feedback for encouraging and guiding student learning remains, and may have increased during that time, and yet there is much evidence of problems and dissatisfaction with many aspects of the assessment process.

Efforts have been made to resolve those problems but they have been made within the established beliefs about the nature and operation of assessment that were founded in higher education of a different era. We need to adopt a different perspective. Although there have been several calls for educational professionals to have a better understanding of assessment, this misses out the other partner in assessment—the student. Examination of the problem by researchers within the UK and across the world points to the importance of supporting students to make judgements about their own work and that of others, to self-regulate, to engage in dialogue with peers and staff, and of developing a greater common understanding of assessment standards. We are sure it is time to look differently at the roles of staff and students within the process and recognise the need for both of them to have a better understanding of assessment processes and standards by developing assessment literacy and acknowledging the importance of their participation in communities of assessment practice to increase and enhance that literacy. This assertion comes from our careful consideration of theory, practice and research over many years

Almost two decades ago we started to question and investigate assessment practices in higher education. At the time, assessment practice seemed to be based on a mix of assumptions, intuition and each tutor's own experience of being assessed. There was limited empirical evidence on which to base claims of consistency and clarity of standards. Our concerns about assessment and assessment standards have been increasingly echoed elsewhere including in the press, in the UK Parliament and through attempts to capture the student view of their higher education experience e.g. the UK National Student Survey. So we have been encouraged to continue asking our questions and to carry out research. We have sought to find out how to make assessment more transparent and thereby help students to understand the quality of work that is required and assure staff that the standards they use are consistent and aligned with those of their colleagues. Our journey has led us to a point where we believe that simple or blanket solutions to the deep-seated problems of assessment and feedback are not the way forward. A more holistic approach is required. This book sets out the approach we believe is necessary to move beyond the quick fix or partial solution of problems, and to bring about a rewarding and demystified approach for students and staff. Fundamentally, we advocate that there is a need for assessment literacy so that both staff and students have expertise and understanding in the domain of assessment. Widespread assessment literacy would inevitably lead to more holistic viewpoints and practice, understanding the interconnectedness of assessment, feedback, community, standards, and self-regulation. However, the importance that assessment literacy is accorded and the resources allocated to its development will reflect the culture and priorities of each institution.

When we started we were at the forefront of developing and using explicit assessment criteria and level descriptors. Our research soon revealed the inadequacy of this approach. Against a tide of acceptance and promotion of the use of criteria and descriptors within the sector we sought more effective methods based both on a theoretical framework and research into practice with our students.

The value and relevance of our work was recognised in 2005 with the award of funding for five years for a Centre for Excellence in Teaching and Learning from the Higher Education Funding Council for England. Named ASKe (Assessment Standards Knowledge exchange), the Centre focused on developing an evidence base and good practice to support HE communities in sharing understandings of assessment standards. The funding enabled us to expand our work and develop it further by working with others. In particular it allowed us to confirm the usefulness of methods we had developed when used in other contexts, to bring together knowledge and evidence about various aspects of assessment and make links between them, and to look at the effects of community participation in developing a shared understanding of assessment and assessment standards.

This work has led us to become convinced that the key is assessment literacy. It is essential for effective assessment practice—and yet it is largely unrecognised. Even where staff undergo training for teaching, the development of their assessment literacy is limited, often only focusing on rules, techniques and use of explicit criteria but not exploring factors such as the tacit nature of standards or the importance of relationships in engaging with feedback. For students, the situation is worse: they usually face a situation where their assessment literacy is either deemed unimportant or, at best, something that will be absorbed, as if by osmosis, as part of navigating their way through the higher education process.

While assessment in the HE system has managed, until recently, to function without much critical examination, the environment is changing, particularly in relation to student expectations of their experience and the part they will be able to play in shaping that experience. There is a still a debate about the nature of the students' role in the HE of the future, as consumer, co-producer, etc., but regardless of its exact nature students will need to make choices about the learning experience being offered to them and which factors are important to them in their learning. It is in their interest and the interest of staff and HEIs that students make those choices from an informed standpoint, informed not just by data but also by understanding of the complexity of learning, teaching and assessment. An assessment literate student will recognise his or her role in assessment and take a different view of issues from an assessment illiterate student.

In seeking to persuade readers of the importance of assessment literacy amongst both staff and students, this book tries to balance the conceptual, the 'how to,' the 'how could' and the 'what if.' So in part it provides theoretical underpinning for the ideas put forward and proposals made, it uses evidence of impact of proposed changes, it puts forward details of how to change practice and discusses the potential of such change to radically reform assessment and feedback. It is firmly based on the work and discussions within the pedagogy research community and proposes theoretical frameworks that are relevant to all HE contexts. There are descriptions of specific successful initiatives that can be emulated directly by practitioners and, in addition, there are reports of interventions made, but not yet fully evaluated, that others may also wish to implement and/or develop further.

Within a changing environment with an increasing emphasis on student involvement this book is intended as a timely contribution that argues that higher education assessment literacy is key to better learning and satisfaction. Institutions, tutors and students not only need to acknowledge that assessment literacy must be clearly understood and developed but also take steps to promote and support it within programmes of study. Greater understanding of assessment processes and standards should lead to better designed assessment and a focus on learning rather than assessment techniques.

Margaret Price

Chris Rust

Berry O'Donovan

Karen Handley

Oxford, March 2012

Acknowledgements

We are very grateful to Rebecca Bryant for working with us to produce this book. Without her it might never have been produced. She displayed patience and forbearance in listening to discussions and, sometimes, disagreements between the authors in the process of refining and clarifying the details of the book.

We would also like to thank Birgit den Outer, Mike Brocklehurst and Belinda Russell, all of whom read an earlier draft and gave us valuable feedback.

Finally, we would like to thank Meg Richardson for advising on production issues, and for doing a very fine job of designing and typesetting the book.

Introduction:
Focus, Aims and Structure

1. The focus of this book

In a nutshell, we believe that:

> For students to reach their potential in terms of their assessed performance, they need to become 'assessment literate', and they need to do this as active participants in the broader education system.

Clearly, this is a strong (and possibly contentious) assertion that requires justification. Throughout this book, we seek to support our claim by:

(1) deconstructing and conceptualising 'assessment literacy' in relation to the roles of both staff and students;

(2) identifying and analysing its main components; and

(3) providing practical guidance for its development.

This book, then, focuses on assessment literacy (and its relationship to learning): how we define it; what it encompasses; and how students can become assessment literate, with the ultimate goal of improving student learning. Its purpose therefore is three-fold:

- To introduce readers (largely staff) to the concept of assessment literacy and how it can be developed.

- To persuade staff of the importance and benefits of assessment literacy, not only for them, but more especially for students, thereby highlighting the role

that staff must play in supporting students to develop
assessment literacy.

- To illustrate that the benefits of assessment literacy
result in better student learning and performance and
less dependency on staff.

Student assessment literacy has become even more important in today's
fee-paying world of higher education in which students play many
more roles and possess power far beyond that of their traditional
(instructed) learner role. For example, students now act as evaluators
of the education they receive (both module-by-module and programme
level); they participate in designing and planning programmes; and,
ultimately and in the longer term, they will act as distributers of
resources through the fees they pay. If students are to be effective
co-producers in higher education, it is imperative that they are
knowledgeable about education and about assessment in particular.

It is also important to note that, although we largely concentrate on
students in this book, those students are part of a broader learning
environment involving staff who also need to be assessment literate.
Put simply: if staff do not understand the basic principles of assessment,
how can we expect students to learn from them and develop their own
assessment literacy? This is an issue for which institutions have
responsibility and it is an issue that we address throughout the course
of the book.

2. Assessment literacy

2.1 Towards a definition

The term 'literacy' has traditionally been used in the context of skills
(e.g. language) and associated with attributes of fluency, competence,
confidence even, and the term also has more subtle connotations
relating to 'gateway' or 'threshold' skills which, once mastered, allow
access to further learning and knowledge. (It is only once someone is
fluent in medical terminology and the techniques of diagnosis, for
example, that they are able to progress to the skills of prescribing and
patient care.) Once across the threshold, one not only possesses the

requisite skills and understanding, but is also able to evaluate a situation and make decisions about which skills should be deployed when and for what purpose[1]. (To continue the metaphor: someone skilled in diagnosis is able to make decisions about appropriate treatments, the benefits of hospitalisation versus home care, and so on.) In our view, it is this latter meaning of the term which is so significant and, throughout this chapter, we will return to the notion of assessment literacy as a gateway or threshold to further learning.

'Assessment' is a term in such common usage that definition could be considered redundant. However, definitions of assessment can be broader or narrower, depending on people's interpretation of them. For example, the QAA definition of assessment as 'any processes that appraise an individual's knowledge, understanding, abilities or skills' (QAA 2006, p.4) can be construed as either broader or narrower, depending on whether one understands 'processes of appraisal' to include formative and summative assessment, or to refer to summative assessment alone. In this book we use 'assessment' not only to refer to the measurement of student achievement, but also to the giving of feedback and the support and promotion of student learning typified by terms such as 'formative assessment', 'assessment for learning', and 'learning-orientated assessment'. In other words, the aim of assessment is to evaluate the quality of the work submitted and to make suggestions for improvement, thereby increasing student understanding of what is expected and promoting improved future performance. It has been repeatedly and convincingly evidenced that assessment is often a significant driver of student learning (Brown and Knight 1994; Ramsden 1992; O'Donovan et al. 2000). Consequently, this broader definition of assessment recognises the need for assessment to motivate and challenge the learner, stimulate learning, and provide feedback. At the same time, assessment must still measure performance—it should test achievement, accredit learning and provide evidence to satisfy quality measures (Price, Carroll et al. 2010).

The term 'assessment literacy' is still in its infancy and is already being used by some authors (see, for example, Baird 2010; Black et al. 2010;

---

[1] See pages 10-11 and footnote 2 for more detail on this distinction.

Broadfoot 2008). However there does not seem to be a generally accepted characterisation of its constituent elements.

We believe that assessment literacy (much like linguistic literacy) involves a combination of knowledge, skills and competencies, including knowledge of a vocabulary and a grammar. And, like linguistic literacy, it goes beyond knowing the meaning of specific words (basic principles) and the rules of grammatical construction (technical approaches)—just as being literate enables one to read and appreciate Shakespeare's plays or Jane Austen's novels, so being assessment literate equips one with an appreciation of the purpose and processes of assessment, which enables one to engage deeply with assessment standards, to make a choice about which skill or which area of knowledge to apply, to appreciate which are/are not appropriate to a particular task, and why. Thus, when assessment literate students undertake an assessment task, they will already be familiar with the appropriate assessment standards; they do not discover the standards through doing the task (although they may well learn more about both the subject and assessment itself by doing the task). In this way, both linguistic and assessment literacy are enablers (gateways or thresholds): they enable one to go beyond a grasp of basic principles towards a deeper understanding and engagement.

More specifically, we believe that assessment literacy encompasses:

- an appreciation of assessment's relationship to learning;
- a conceptual understanding of assessment (i.e. understanding of the basic principles of valid assessment and feedback practice, including the terminology used);
- understanding of the nature, meaning and level of assessment criteria and standards;
- skills in self- and peer assessment;
- familiarity with technical approaches to assessment (i.e. familiarity with pertinent assessment and feedback skills, techniques, and methods, including their purpose and efficacy); and

- possession of the intellectual ability to select and apply appropriate approaches and techniques to assessed tasks (not only does one have the requisite skills, but one is also able to judge which skill to use when, for which task)[2].

Furthermore, we believe that assessment literacy is closely linked with other literacies—academic, pedagogic and digital, for example: literacy in all of these interlinked areas contributes to successful learning. And finally (as sketched above), we believe that assessment literacy is an enabler or gateway/threshold—once a student starts to become assessment literate, they are in a position to progress, increase their learning, and perform more effectively. (If, through a marking exercise, a student better understands how to build a structured argument, for example, they are in a position to apply that understanding in their assessed work, to build more complex arguments, to apply that skill to other areas of their life, to impart their understanding to others, etc.)

2.2 The case for assessment literacy

Why, then, should we promote assessment literacy among students and staff? It seems that assessment literacy improves students' assessed performance (see Price, Carroll et al. 2010). Indeed, it seems obvious that the more students know about what is being asked of them in assessments, the more effectively they will be able to meet those requirements[3]. Assessment lies at the centre of the student experience, it is a dominant influence on student learning, and students are keen to know how to improve. As Brown and Knight (1994, p.7) state: 'Assessment defines what the students regard as important, how they

[2] In the development of his seminal taxonomy of the cognitive domain, Bloom (1956) distinguished between 'intellectual skills' (techniques for solving problems) and 'intellectual abilities' (selecting which information or technique should be used). This is the precise distinction that we are drawing in bullet points 5 and 6 above (familiarity with technical approaches vs. the ability to select from amongst those approaches). Eljamal et al. (1997, p.7) further corroborate this point: 'Research on student intellectual growth in higher education, particularly students' own reports, has helped research to distinguish this process of recognising and abstracting relationships from that of developing cognitive skills.'

[3] Some may argue that this simply teaches students 'to the test', but this only becomes as issue when assessment tasks are poorly designed—more detail is given on this point later in this section in relation to Miller and Parlett's (1974) work on cue aware students.

spend their time and how they come to see themselves as students and then as graduates.' As a result, much has been written about how to improve assessment practice, and much has been implemented, but often this has involved a piecemeal approach (see the introduction to Havnes and McDowell (2008) for a setting of the scene)—failing to appreciate the 'big picture' by, for example, not recognising that innovative methods employed on one module (allocating students to learning sets, for example) may well be adopted and transferred to another module by the students themselves (students benefitting from continuing to work in those learning sets, even though this is not part of the formal learning process in this module). And, despite all this effort, student satisfaction ratings for assessment and feedback remain obstinately poor in most HE contexts, particularly with regard to how effectively assessment and feedback practices support students in improving their academic performance.

Where learning is focused on memorisation and reproduction, assessment may seem more straightforward. Feedback can be clear and specific; less nuanced and contextual. In such binary contexts, the association between student effort and results is more explicit, and students generally see assessment as both fair and transparent: work hard and you will do well. However, in tertiary education, where knowledge is much more likely to be contested and high-level, complex learning is demanded. This means that reproducing the knowledge and understanding of others is not enough. Interpretation is required, achievement is often a 'matter of degree' (as opposed to an absolute), and a variety of responses to assessed tasks may be considered excellent. This not only makes it more difficult to give a clear definition of what constitutes high-quality work, but also means that the link between effort and marks awarded becomes more tenuous. Marking processes may seem unfair. A student who equates effort with marks may think: 'I have worked hard and still not achieved an A grade—something must be wrong with the teaching'—and it is not difficult to understand this logic of the assessment illiterate student.

Until now, most attempts to improve assessment and feedback have, perhaps understandably, focused on getting the tutor-designed mechanics of assessment 'right'. Quality assurance and student satisfaction surveys have directed our attention towards reliability—explicit and measurable objectives in the assessment process, such as explicitness and clarity of criteria, timeliness of feedback, alignment with learning outcomes, etc. These are all laudable objectives, but, as illustrated by the critical student in the paragraph above, getting the mechanics and design of assessment right (whatever 'right' means and however difficult that task) is a necessary but not sufficient condition for fundamentally improving assessment practice, including students' assessed performance and their satisfaction.

Not only do the mechanics of assessment need to be right, but students need to understand the rationale for the selected assessment design, as well as the quality characteristics that tutors seek in their assessed work—they need to have crossed the assessment literacy threshold (or passed through its gateway) in order to engage with the standards at this deeper level. As Sadler (1989, p.121) explains, an indispensable condition for students doing well is that they have the same understanding as their tutor of what constitutes a good assignment, so that they can imbue their work with the requisite qualities 'in the act of production itself'. Boud (2007) goes even further, suggesting that not only do students require such self-evaluative abilities within their academic context, but the ability to make informed judgements about one's own work and that of one's peers is an important graduate attribute and employability skill.

It is worth mentioning that, on the face of it, Miller and Parlett's 1974 study of cue awareness amongst students appears to support Sadler's point (above). This study indicated that 'cue seekers' (students who make an effort to find out from their lecturers what kinds of questions will be set in the exams) tend to perform better than the 'cue conscious' (those who listen for, and act on, tips from their lecturers) who, in turn, tend to perform better than the 'cue deaf' (those who simply don't recognise any such cues). However, whilst an assessment literate student may well display cue seeking behaviours they display a broader understanding of assessment and its role in their learning. The Miller and Parlett study fails to take into account the quality of the assessment design. A poorly-designed assessment task which, for example, allows high marks to be awarded for the regurgitation of lecture notes clearly enables cue seeking students to perform well. An assessment literate student would also recognise these cues but also the limitations of the assessment design itself. Thus a cue seeking student does not fully equate to an assessment literate one.

The benefits of assessment literacy may not, however, be immediately obvious to authority-dependent students who are motivated by certainty and believe that the duty of infallible assessors is to 'correct' student work (Baxter Magolda 1992; King and Kitchener 2004). Such students believe the purpose of assessment to be measurement alone, and do not entertain the possibility of assessment for learning. Indeed, assessment illiterate students may simply consider less authority-dependent assessment processes (such as peer review and peer assessment) ingenious ways for lazy tutors to shirk their marking responsibilities or, as in a recent, high-profile, UK student complaint case, university cost cutting (Newman 2009). There are clearly some major hurdles to overcome when developing assessment literacy coherently and effectively.

We opened this section with the question: 'Why, then, should we promote assessment literacy among students and staff?', and we have concentrated on student assessment literacy, since students are the primary focus of this book. However, as we noted at the beginning of this chapter, staff as well as students need to be assessment literate—this is key to the professionalization of higher education that has been taking place in recent years—and the assessment literacy of staff is something that should be addressed via professional development. Indeed, research conducted by Graham Gibbs and Martin Coffey (Gibbs and Coffey 2004) showed that after receiving teacher training, university lecturers were rated by their students significantly more positively on every aspect of teaching quality than previously. In addition, those who had received teacher training became more student-focused over time, whereas their colleagues who had not received such training became significantly less student-focused.

2.3 Developing assessment literacy

We have made the case for promoting assessment literacy in the section above, but how, in actuality, might we go about doing this? Some students become assessment literate, seemingly serendipitously. A typical assessment process, supported by fairly repetitive assessment tasks/practices—whereby motivated students submit assignments, receive written feedback, and in response try different approaches—can, over the long term and mainly through a process of trial and error, enable some students to understand assessment processes, criteria and standards (O'Donovan et al. 2004).

However, it is not at all obvious how to actively encourage development of the kind of assessment literacy required in higher education. Students' assessment experience in secondary education is not usually a good guide to assessment in higher education. This is due to a host of fundamental changes in expectation and learning environment, such as level of autonomy and contact time. But arguably the most fundamental change lies in epistemology. As formally demonstrated by Perry's stages of cognitive development, describing the growth over time of students' epistemologies from dualist through to relativist (Perry 1970; 1981), knowledge tends to become less certain, more contestable and contextual as we rise up the education ladder, even in the sciences. Assessment becomes, correspondingly, less about measuring what you know and more about guiding and judging how knowledge is selected and applied to novel, often ill-structured, situations and problems (King and Kitchener 1994). Assessment processes and criteria in secondary education may be different, and standards definitely should be different, from those in higher education. In order to be successful, students must understand the rules of the new game. We therefore argue that the development of assessment literacy amongst students in higher education must take place early on in their programmes and must involve intentionality in action. In other words, in order to develop assessment literacy, students must actively seek an understanding of what they ought to be doing in relation to assessment and why. They need to examine the nature of the assessment task, grasp its purpose and the various possible ways of responding to it. They need to see how it relates to the rest of the course and their learning, and need to engage with and use feedback.

Advocating a more intentional process for developing student assessment literacy in today's HE context is not easy, and it requires that staff are assessment literate. However, increasing student numbers and diversity, limited resources, and the potential for highly consumerist attitudes amongst students mean that to cope with, or counter, such changes we not only need to share understandings of assessment effectively, but also quickly and inclusively. As Snowdon (2002) acknowledges, there is a cost in terms of time and resource to codifying and sharing knowledge—and this cost increases the more diverse an audience's experience and language.[4] Tsoukas (2003) goes further, arguing that tacit knowledge can never really be codified or made explicit.

Not only are today's undergraduates and postgraduates increasingly heterogeneous, but what also becomes clear from prior research is that students in one discipline can experience a totally different set of understandings of 'quality' in relation to their work from students in another. As Donald (2009) argues, engineering students focus on problem solving using mathematics and the physical sciences, while law students grapple with paradoxes, and students of English literature are required both to be creative and embed their understanding in what has gone before. How assessment literacy is applied and developed varies subtly from discipline to discipline (due to different epistemologies; different techniques and ways of applying them) and there may well be 'issues of translation' when defining 'quality' or setting standards across disciplines. Clearly all students battle with high-level and complex issues which are not quickly or easily learnt, and therefore require coherent development across units of study in aligned programmes of study. But it is seldom sufficient to communicate these understandings simply by 'telling', however carefully considered the wording. Here, we should declare our social constructivist take on learning which becomes increasingly evident in the rest of the book.

2.4 More than just telling

The effective sharing of assessment criteria, standards and processes requires more than just telling, and this is so in a number of ways. First, as will be discussed in detail in Chapter 2, explicit methods of sharing knowledge and understandings are limited—merely telling students what matters in assessment, while valuable, is unlikely to be effective.

---

[4] See Chapter 2, section 3.2 for more detail on this point.

The nature of 'excellence' in a business report, essay, or dissertation, for example, is frustratingly difficult to articulate clearly and unambiguously. Several issues block clear communication, including different interpretations of particular qualities or criteria. For example, if we ask ten individuals within the same discipline to explicitly define 'criticality' or 'analysis', it is likely that we will end up with multiple different definitions—and the more diverse the group (in terms of nationality, discipline, educational experience, etc.), the more diverse the interpretations (O'Donovan et al. 2004).

Unambiguous articulation of 'standards' proves even more slippery. How easy is it to describe the difference in 'good' analysis between undergraduate and postgraduate level or even between a grade C or grade B+ within the same level? When we make an attempt, we inevitably fall back on relative terms such as 'deeper' and 'more complex', or we invoke relative concepts such as the degree of student autonomy involved in the analysis. Relative terms and concepts similarly require articulation of the benchmarks or anchor points to which they refer (Sadler 1987). As a result, we often end up with explanations which are too cumbersome and detailed for the purpose of clear communication. They attain precision only at the cost of practical utility, and this is 'likely to prove counter-productive' (Yorke 2002, p.155).

2.5 Student engagement and participation: the relational dynamic

What, then, does the effective sharing of assessment criteria, standards and processes involve—beyond just telling? Tacit understandings of assessment standards and criteria (the understandings that we find difficult to articulate in words) are shared through social processes involving practice, observation and imitation (Nonaka 1991). This sharing is achieved more effectively in relational communities where the density of interactions between students and staff, staff and staff, and students and students is enhanced. It is therefore perhaps not surprising that large-scale research (involving 25,000 students and 300 institutions) in the US found student involvement (in terms of staff, and particularly peer, interaction) to be the environmental variable that was the most significant in terms of student satisfaction and academic success (Astin 1993).

The importance of interaction with academics and other students cannot be underestimated. Baxter Magolda and King's (2004) work on learning partnerships also stresses the importance of enabling students to share authority and expertise with their peers, thus transforming them from dependent to autonomous agents. Even when we look at the university experience in broader terms, research indicates that departments considered excellent in both research and teaching are synonymous with those where students are drawn into the academic community and work/interact with academics in less authority-dependent ways (Gibbs et al. 2007).[5]

We are not, however, arguing simply for the democratisation of learning environments. In assessment contexts in which summative marks are given, there is (and will always need to be) a clear divide between assessor and assessed. Indeed it is not unreasonable for students themselves to expect that they will receive expert judgement and advice. And this is despite the increasing use of less hierarchical terms to describe the relationship between universities and their students, such as 'consumers', 'active participants', 'co-producers', 'partners', 'community of learning' and 'apprentices' (McCulloch 2009). The National Student Forum (2009, p.6) reports that students now expect to be 'an active partner' in the design and management of 'my education', where their learning is 'personalised to my needs', assessment and feedback is used to 'help me learn'. All of this points to the thirst for a more personalised learning environment (Becket and Brookes 2009)—and this is an environment in which the role of 'novice' and 'expert' can, and must, still exist (although the nature of 'expertise' is more nebulous and difficult to articulate).

Our aim is to make the case for recognising and understanding the influence of the relational dynamic in learning and particularly in feedback.[6] Although learning is still sometimes depicted as a solitary activity undertaken in monastic libraries with weighty and worthy tomes, interaction between the learner and the learned has long been

---

[5] See Chapter 7 of this book for a detailed account of academic communities of practice.

[6] In this case, the relational dynamic is narrow—one-to-one, marker to student, but in Chapter 7 on community we will see that the relational dynamic can also be construed broadly, involving many individuals, both staff and students.

seen as central to the learning process. It is therefore interesting (surprising even) that in many university contexts assessment and feedback are separate, unidirectional, and anonymous processes. The student submits her work to a drop box or administrator and the work is de-identified. The assessor then marks the work 'objectively', writes feedback—perhaps using a standardised template, and subsequently the student is allowed to collect the work—again via an administrative process that disconnects the student from the assessor. In this (stereotypical) situation, there is little opportunity for dialogue between student and assessor about why the student has responded to the assessment task in a particular way, or why the assessor has responded to the submitted work as they have.

In contrast, research undertaken in a three-year FDTL project on engaging students with assessment feedback demonstrated the importance of a relational dialogue between staff and students (Price, Handley et al. 2010). Not only do students benefit from being able to discuss their work, particularly in contexts in which there is no single right way of completing a task, but they are also more likely to treat seriously feedback from those they know and respect. As Mann (2001) points out, when assignments become mere outputs to be produced, the result can be alienation rather than engagement.

2.6 Coherent programme approaches

Not only do we argue for understanding the influence of the relational dynamic in learning, but also for an explicit, coherent and holistic approach to learning. A programme that consists of 20 different units of study, all with different approaches to assessment and feedback, is unlikely to build assessment literacy in a coherent and structured fashion. In order to be effective and achieve multiple purposes, assessment and feedback practices require holistic approaches, and especially alignment at programme level.[7] Furthermore, any programme-level approaches require that all staff involved in the programme understand explicitly the assessment literacy embedded in

---

[7] See Chapter 3 of this book for a detailed discussion of approaches to assessment at programme level.

that programme.[8] This is perhaps best achieved in institutions that embed common pedagogic values. One such example is Alverno College in the US, which embodies a radical, outcome-based pedagogy that affects and connects every aspect of the college, but particularly its curriculum design, teaching and assessment. Alverno has the development of assessment (and pedagogic) literacy very much at its heart, emphasising self- and peer assessment, concern for the emotional domain, and the importance of students understanding how they learn. Clearly, disciplinary differences in terms of subject and critical thinking exist, but every member of staff and every student at Alverno is cognizant of the overarching pedagogic approach from the time of their entry to the college—and, since this approach is systemic and highly structured, all college members develop a deep understanding of the Alverno pedagogy over time.[9]

Similarly, PBL (problem-based learning)—particularly used in applied disciplines (medicine, nursing, engineering, etc.)—adopts a student-centred, problem-solving approach to learning which cuts across disciplines and encourages the development of generic, lifelong learning skills. Under the PBL model, students work together in small teams to define, discuss and resolve real-world problems. By definition, these problems are ill-structured and there is no one correct solution to them. As students work to resolve a problem, they gather more information that shapes both the problem and the solution, and they are, in parallel, developing skills of team working, collaboration, independent thinking, problem solving and critical analysis—all of which are essential for life outside higher education. In the process of solving problems and developing further skills, these students are also learning and honing the skill of assessment literacy. Under the PBL model, the role of lecturer/tutor thus changes from that of dispenser of information to that of mentor, guide and coach. Not only does PBL

---

[8] Although the examples we give below relate to traditional modes of learning, it is also important that coherent approaches are applied to non-traditional modes, such as distance learning, and that non-traditional learners receive appropriate support in this area—via personal tutors, for instance.

[9] See *Student Assessment-as-Learning at Alverno College* (1994) for a detailed exposition of the Alverno approach.

encourage assessment literacy amongst students, but it also demands that staff are assessment literate in relation to the PBL methodology.[10]

3.   The structure of this book

In the preceding sections of this chapter, we set out the main focus and aims of this book. We also defined 'assessment literacy' and emphasised the key role of the gateway or threshold which, once passed through, enables students to engage with assessment standards at a deep level, to understand the purpose and nature of assessment tasks, and to select appropriate approaches to them. We claimed that in order to maximise their learning and assessed performance, students must be assessment literate and this, in turn, requires a holistic approach and a relational dynamic between staff and students.

In the following chapters we put meat on the bones of these claims. We set out our own theoretical standpoint and discuss in detail what assessment literacy means for all stages of the assessment process—pre-, during and post-assessment. We also give some practical examples of how assessment literacy can be developed at different stages of the process.

The chapters of this book can be read in two ways—either as standalone units (for those who are interested in specific aspects of assessment literacy), or in sequence from start to finish (for those who are interested in gaining an understanding of assessment literacy in its entirety). For those who fall into the former category, cross references are provided at appropriate points so that readers may refer to parts of other chapters for further information, more detail, or related points.

Chapter 2, then, is theoretical, and showcases our own models of how students (and staff) come to know assessment standards, as well as providing a brief history of other models that have been proposed in relation to the sharing of assessment standards.

The remaining chapters of the book focus on the practicalities of carrying out assessment. Chapter 3 considers the planning of

---

[10] For a full introduction to problem-based learning, see, for example, Savin Boden and Howell Major 2004.

assessment. It promotes a programme-level approach to planning assessment and explores the kinds of decisions that need to be made prior to planning a programme-level assessment strategy.

In Chapter 4 we discuss pre-assessment activity, exploring the kinds of techniques and exercises that staff can use to prepare students for assessment and to increase their assessment literacy. We focus in particular on our own widely adopted assessment intervention which uses a marking exercise and workshop to develop student understanding of assessment criteria.

Chapter 5 looks at assessment activity mainly from the perspective of staff. Although staff engage students in assessment activity (both formative and summative) and support that engagement in a range of ways, there are two particular points that we focus on: firstly when staff choose the type of assessment activity or task that they will set for their students, and secondly when staff mark their students' responses to the assessment task set. This chapter therefore covers both these aspects of staff involvement in assessment activity and also considers the importance of self- and peer review while undertaking the assessment task.

Chapter 6 focuses on post-assessment activity, or feedback. We consider the nature and purpose of feedback, and discuss how students can be encouraged to engage more effectively with their assessment feedback. We also introduce our own analytical stages of engagement model, which depicts the various stages of engagement within the feedback process including points of and reasons for disengagement.

And finally, Chapter 7 explores the fundamental notion of community, which underlies all stages of the assessment and learning process. In this chapter we attempt to define community, explain why it is so important to focus on encouraging a sense of community, and consider some of the ways in which a community of practice can be cultivated drawn from our own experience at Oxford Brookes University.

Chapter 8 provides an overview of the key points of the book and, in so doing, summarises our claims and justification about the importance of assessment literacy.

A Theoretical Perspective: a Matrix and a Cultivated Community of Practice Model

1. Introduction

In the previous chapter we defined assessment literacy and stressed the fundamental role that it plays in maximising student learning and assessed performance. In order to cultivate assessment literacy we argued that it is necessary to adopt a holistic approach, to foster a relational dynamic between staff and students, and to recognise that learning needs to be less authority-dependent than has traditionally been assumed.

Given that this is our approach, the question becomes: how, in reality, can we develop assessment literacy amongst the student body? In order to answer this question, we need to examine the theory underpinning our approach. We look at the kind of theoretical models that we need to adopt in order to create an environment that is conducive to assessment literacy amongst today's students.

In the first instance, however, it is vital to appreciate the importance that assessment standards play in the development of assessment literacy. It is only once an individual fully understands the assessment standards, i.e. the standards against which their work will be assessed, that they can make a judgement about how best to approach and produce a piece of work for assessment. An understanding of standards is also required for an individual to undertake effective self- and peer assessment. A full understanding of the nature of assessment standards is therefore one of the pre-requisites for assessment literacy, and it is for this reason that we focus on standards in this chapter, prior to examining other, broader aspects of assessment literacy in later chapters. Indeed, as we will see later in the chapter, our own models of how individuals come to know assessment standards lead to a more complex understanding of standards, hence a broader understanding of assessment literacy.

This chapter has three main purposes. First, it showcases our own models of how students (and staff) come to know assessment standards. Second, it provides a brief history of other models that have been proposed in relation to the sharing of assessment standards. Third, it makes clear through this juxtaposition that out own approach retains a number of features of the preceding historical approaches; there is a logical progression from earlier approaches to our own. This chapter thus sets our position within the academic landscape, as well as enabling readers to understand how our thinking has developed over time and why our approach incorporates the characteristics that it does.

We propose two interrelated models. The first is an overarching model and is depicted as a 'matrix' which indicates progress through the various historical approaches to assessment up to our own 'cultivated community of practice' approach. The second, the 'cultivated community of practice' model, is our own model of how students come to know assessment standards. It indicates via two interconnected cycles how we believe the assessment process should work (including feedback back and forth between the two cycles) in order to maximise assessment literacy amongst both students and staff.

2.   The matrix

We believe that previous approaches to understanding how assessment standards are shared can be categorised into three types of model:

- the traditional model
- the explicit model; and
- the social constructivist model.

Each of these models is different from the other and has a set of distinct, defining features (each model is discussed in detail below). We have argued that there has also been a historical progress from one model to the next, beginning with the traditional and ending with the social constructivist. We have set these models out in a matrix (see figure 2.1 below), with the traditional model occupying quadrant 1 of the matrix, the explicit occupying quadrant 2 and the social constructivist occupying quadrant 3. These approaches are defined in the matrix by whether the inputs and activities involved are formal or informal, and by the degree of active student engagement in the processes. The curved arrow indicates the historical progress through the models, from past to future. Finally, quadrant 4 is occupied by our own cultivated community of practice model, which we set out in detail in section 3.4 below.

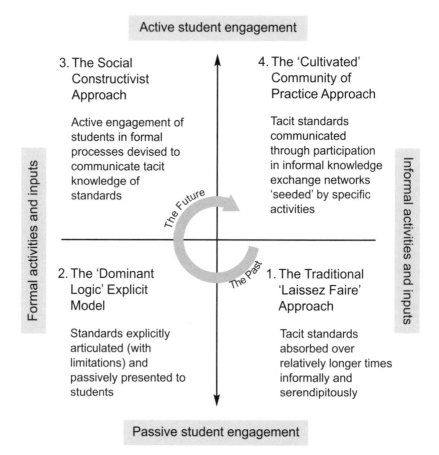

Figure 2.1: Approaches to developing student understanding of assessment standards

The matrix is a very useful device in that not only does it depict previous approaches to the sharing of assessment standards, but it also illustrates one of the key features of our own cultivated community of practice model. That is, that our model retains and incorporates elements from the previous models—it does not mark a complete departure from all aspects of previous models. So, for example, the cultivated community of practice model acknowledges the importance of explicit articulation of assessment standards (as does the explicit model); and it acknowledges the importance of actively engaging students in formal processes designed to communicate tacit knowledge of assessment standards (as does the social constructivist model). Our cultivated community of practice model, then, can be seen as the culmination of previous models. (And, in fact, quadrants 2, 3 and 4 of the matrix each embody the understandings of the preceding model, as set out in the matrix cycle.)

In the following sections we will discuss in detail all four models of the sharing of assessment standards, as depicted in the matrix. We will look at the key characteristics as well as the disadvantages of the three historical models and thereby explain which features of those models are retained in our own cultivated community of practice model, and why.

3. Approaches to sharing assessment standards

3.1 The traditional model (matrix quadrant 1)

It has been argued that, in the past (and prior to the massification of higher education), academic communities were more stable, homogenous and close-knit (Ecclestone 2001). Academic departments were smaller, most of their staff were tenured, and those staff taught far fewer students than today, all of which gave rise to greater opportunities for frequent, enduring interactions between both staff members, and staff and their students. In addition, academic programmes were less fragmented than today (Winter 1994)—components ran over longer time periods, and students were taught in smaller numbers by more constant staff.

Within this context, the traditional model of sharing assessment standards assumes that students come to know assessment standards gradually, over time. These standards are not explicitly set out for, or taught to, students. Rather, students become acquainted with standards almost serendipitously through trial and error, via feedback and informal discussions with their tutors about the nature and values of their subject. Significantly, under the traditional model, knowledge of the nature and standards of assessment is not really considered (or is not considered worthy to be?) separate from subject-specific knowledge: what is important is gaining knowledge of one's subject, and the successful student simply picks up the talent of performing well under assessed conditions as (s)he goes along.

Arguably, there exist institutions in which the traditional model still applies. The Oxford tutorial system, for instance, fits the bill of very small group (one-on-one or one-on-two) teaching, in which students develop a close relationship with their tutor over time and benefit from extensive discussion about their subject and detailed feedback on their work. This relationship is further strengthened by students and staff living in close proximity in college, which affords further opportunities for informal interactions. However, one of the key disadvantages of the traditional model is that it fails to provide an adequate explanation of how students come to know assessment standards and is not transferable to today's mainstream student environment of ever-increasing student numbers, with resulting large class sizes and minimal staff–student interaction.

An important aspect of the traditional model (as touched on above), and indeed its second disadvantage, is the lack of explicitness regarding standards. In fact, assessment judgements are shrouded in mystery and considered to be the sole domain of tutors, based on their tacit professional expertise. Individual tutors' assessment judgements are thought indisputable and assessment is seen as an art—something akin to wine tasting or tea blending (O'Donovan et al. 2004). Getting assessment right is a feeling, a sixth sense rather than a rational decision that can be articulated clearly to the uninitiated layman. Consequently, it is not seen as necessary to provide information about assessment standards or assessment processes and few formal mechanisms exist for such provision within the traditional model—and that knowledge therefore remains completely tacit. However, in today's HE environment, where the government calls for clear articulation of standards, clear justification of grades/marks awarded, and public accountability, this is a major failing: the traditional approach simply cannot provide an adequate model of the sharing of assessment standards for either staff or students.

The Traditional Model

Key features

- Depends on small student numbers & prolonged student–staff interaction
- Assessment standards considered tacit and implicit in subject with little or no attempt to make them explicit
- Strong sense of tutor as expert & beyond question

Disadvantages

Inapplicable in today's HE environment because:

- Large classes & limited student–staff interaction are the norm
- Public and policymakers demand explicit standards and accountability

---

3.2 The explicit model (matrix quadrant 2)

Over the past 30+ years (since the 1980s) academic communities have clearly become more fragmented. Academic departments are much larger and employ significant numbers of staff on short-term contracts as well as part-time, hourly paid lecturers, with these staff moving on to new contracts elsewhere quite regularly. This means that staff have far fewer opportunities for sharing assessment standards and criteria amongst themselves—there is less of a close-knit staff 'community' and some staff (e.g. part-time, hourly paid) may only be present in the institution when they are actually teaching a class. Student numbers have grown correspondingly over the past two decades, with modular programmes becoming increasingly common. The result has been larger and larger classes, ever-diminishing contact time between staff and students, and lack of staff continuity for students. Consequently, opportunities for sharing assessment standards between staff and students have also been heavily eroded—and students and staff have, as a default position, been driven towards explicit standards and taking an individual approach to their learning as a result of the lack of opportunity to interact within an academic community. As we saw in the preceding section, in today's world of mass higher education, short-term contracts and staff mobility, the traditional model of sharing assessment standards can no longer hold. (We might further observe that over the past 30+ years there has been a general move throughout the public sector towards quality assurance and accountability, in response to public demand for transparency in areas such as the NHS and local government.)

The impact of these changes has been recognised, both by academic researchers and policy makers, and concern has been growing regarding marking reliability and standards (at the time of writing most recently exemplified in the UK by the Select Committee Report). There has been a corresponding move towards formalising and codifying assessment standards by course and discipline via the adoption of learning outcomes, disciplinary benchmark statements and increasing adherence to explicit systems and procedures (Winter 1994).

On the face of it, the explicit model appears to answer the problem of lack of opportunity for students to gain knowledge of assessment standards. If knowledge can no longer be gained through prolonged, informal interactions, then the obvious solution seems to be to set out what is required clearly and simply so that it can be examined and absorbed by anyone who cares to look. Indeed, we, too, believed explicit articulation to be the answer when in 1996/7, in an attempt to more effectively clarify assessment standards for learners, we created a criterion referenced assessment grid for use by both staff and students across the Business School at Oxford Brookes University (Price and Rust 1999; O'Donovan et al. 2000). The grid is still widely used within the School and elsewhere and sets out grade descriptors for each grade against each criterion used in the assessment of undergraduate work (see figure 2.2 overleaf for selected examples). This enables suitable criteria to be selected for each assessment task and equips both students and assessors with information about the standards applied for each criterion. We hoped that this would be a straightforward means of ensuring the consistent application of standards by markers and of clarifying standards to guide student learning.

Unfortunately, our hopes did not match reality. Students either did not refer to the information provided or could not satisfactorily interpret it.

7029 Placement Search and Preparation - Feedback Sheet

ASSIGNMENT 1

	CRITERION	A	B+
1	Presentation of assignment	Shows a polished and imaginative approach to the topic	Carefully and logically organised
7	Attention to purpose	Has addressed the purpose of the assignment comprehensively and imaginatively	Has addressed the purpose of the assignment coherently and with some attempt to demonstrate imagination
27	Self-criticism (include reflection on practice)	Is confident in application of own criteria of judgement and in challenge of received opinion in action and can reflect on action	Is able to evaluate own strengths and weaknesses; can challenge received opinion and begins to develop own criteria and judgement
28	Independence/ Autonomy (include planning and managing learning)	With minimum guidance can manage own learning using full range of resources for discipline; can seek and make use of feedback	Identifies strengths of learning needs and follows activities to improve performance; is autonomous in straightforward study tasks

(Please tick boxes)

Comment: ....

....

....

Student Name:

Student Number:

B	C	Refer/Fail
Shows organisation and coherence	Shows some attempt to organise in a logical manner	Disorganised/incoherent
Has addressed the main purpose of the assignment	Some of the work is focused on the aims and themes of the assignment	Fails to address the task set
Is largely dependent on criteria set by others but begins to recognise own strengths and weaknesses	Dependent on criteria set by others. Begins to recognise own strengths and weakness	Fails to meaningfully undertake the process of self criticism
Can work independently within a relevant ethos and can access and use a range of learning resources	Can undertake clearly directed work independently within a relevant ethos and, with some guidance, use the standard learning resources	Unable to work independently, needing significant guidance on methods and resources

Marker: Mark:

Figure 2.2: A limited example of an assessment grid

Student focus group participants[1] pointed out that greater clarification of the terms and phrases used in the grid was required ('...I mean 'address them comprehensively' what do you mean'), and that the interpretation of words and their meanings are always subjective, hence terminology is open to multiple interpretations by individual staff and students ('[it's] open to interpretation—what some might perceive as imaginative, other people may not'). However, there was widespread agreement that, despite the practical problems of using the grid, it was a good idea. The students clearly welcomed a more systematic marking process and appreciated what the grid was trying to achieve ('I think its aims and objectives are very good and it could help students a lot') (O'Donovan et al. 2000, pp.79-81).

In an effort to address the issues highlighted in the focus groups, and to limit the need for interpretation, we initially considered trying to specify the assessment criteria using even tighter language. However, we soon realised that this would not work. The more precisely you try to define something, the more you risk using specialised terminology, thus making it even less likely that your audience will understand. In addition, if you increase the quantity of explanation, you are likely to end up with descriptors that are unwieldy and difficult to use. Finally (and perhaps most importantly), verbal descriptions of assessment standards do not stand alone. They require an understanding of the surrounding context and are, by nature, vague. For example, the term 'reasonably coherent' does not have an absolute meaning that applies across the board. Its meaning is (partially) dictated by the assessor's expectations and knowledge of the context (e.g. what can be expected from a first year as opposed to a third year; whether the students have undertaken this kind of analysis before; the assessor's experience of previous assessment tasks in this area). Ultimately, under the explicit model, each grade descriptor has to be worked out anew for each assessment in order that each descriptor accurately reflects the relevant expectations and context. Clearly, this is unworkable in practice. We, like Snowdon (2002), recognise that there is a cost (both in time and resource) involved in codifying knowledge that stems from the need to create a shared context amongst

[1] We undertook an initial broad sweep survey by questionnaire to gain an overview of the student experience of the use and effectiveness of the criterion assessment grid. We then used this data to structure conversational style 'prompts' which were given to a number of student focus groups in order to gather more qualitative, in-depth data.

all stakeholders, and this cost increases relative to the stakeholders' inexperience and lack of acquaintance with technical language.

So, while the current dominant logic of UK HE focuses on explicit articulation of standards, this is not sufficient in practice. What, then, is missing and what can we do to fill this gap? As touched on in section 3.1 above, it all comes back to tacit knowledge—no matter how precisely and explicitly you articulate standards, there will always remain a body of tacit knowledge and experience that does not easily lend itself to articulation and explanation. This tacit knowledge has to be acquired by another means. In the words of Sadler (1987, p.199), assessment standards reside 'essentially in unarticulated form inside the heads of assessors and are normally transferred expert to novice by joint participation in evaluative activity'.

The Explicit Model

Key features

- Explicitly articulates assessment standards & criteria
- Provides a systematic approach to assessment
- Responds to national concern about standards & reliability of marking
- Reflects today's HE environment of large classes & limited student–staff interaction

Disadvantages

- Difficulty of unambiguously defining terms
- Ignores tacit dimension of knowledge

3.3 The social constructivist model (matrix quadrant 3)

If explicit articulation is not the answer, then we need to look elsewhere for inspiration. We perhaps need to look towards Sadler's 'joint participation in evaluative activity', mentioned above. The social constructivist model promotes a form of active learning whereby stakeholders come to know assessment standards through use and application, thereby enabling them to create their own meaning within their own personal and cognitive constructs (Vygotsky 1978). Tacit knowledge is thus developed via use of, and increasing familiarity with, the standards. This is clearly a more student-centred approach, in which students become active participants in the learning process rather than static recipients of knowledge, leading to the need for more complex/sophisticated assessment literacy. Lea and Street's (1998) 'academic socialisation' approach, in which the tutor's role is to induct students into the praxis of the academic community, is one example of the social constructivist model.

In developing and adapting our assessment grid research (above), we undertook a further research project aimed at enhancing students' understanding of assessment criteria and processes through a structured intervention involving transfer of both tacit and explicit knowledge (Rust et al. 2003). This was, effectively, a 'test' of the social constructivist model. The study, undertaken with large classes (300+) of students in the Business School at Oxford Brookes University, showed that performance can improve significantly when students are engaged, prior to any formal assessment, in activities designed to support the social construction of knowledge of assessment criteria and standards. These activities included consideration of exemplars, practice marking, and small-group and tutor-led discussion of criteria and standards.

Specifically, the study (or intervention) took place in the final three weeks of the students' first term on a Business degree programme. It involved the students in preparation work (each independently completing mark sheets for two sample assignments), participation at a 90-minute workshop (involving small group discussion of the sample assignment marking; feedback to the plenary; tutor-led discussion and explanation; small group review of marking in light of tutor explanation; final reports on grades from small groups to plenary; and tutor provision and explanation of marked sample assignments), and submission (three weeks later, at the end of the first term) of a self-assessment sheet along with their coursework.

Our findings, which were measured over three consecutive years, showed that students who undertook the optional 90-minute pre-assessment workshop demonstrated a significant improvement in their performance in assessed tasks compared to those who did not undertake the workshop. (This held even though baseline comparison of participants and non-participants undertaken prior to the intervention indicated no significant difference in performance at that stage.) Furthermore, one year later, participants in the intervention continued to demonstrate improved performance, albeit at a slightly reduced level.[2]

This research illustrates that coming to know assessment standards involves both explicit and tacit knowledge (the latter being gained through use of, and discussion about, the standards). While explicit articulation of standards does have a role to play (while students could see that the assessment grid discussed in section 3.2 above was, to a certain extent, beneficial), what makes the difference is having the opportunity to discuss and use those standards via an active learning process involving both students and tutor (as demonstrated by the results of the assessment intervention and workshop in the preceding paragraph). Students seem, quite quickly, to absorb the processes and standards in this way—and this has an immediate as well as a longer-lasting effect, giving a broader understanding of assessment standards and thereby increasing assessment literacy. The social constructivist model, then, appears to work—but it is important to note that in this model, the tutor still retains the role of expert and it is his/her voice that holds sway.

The Social Constructivist Model

Key features

- Student-centred, active learning approach
- Recognises limitation of explicit transfer methods
- Tacit knowledge gradually realised through engagement with standards
- Tutor sets formal exercises to facilitate absorption of explicit and tacit knowledge

Disadvantages

- Inequality between student & tutor (tutor remains authoritative)
- Student lacks proactive role (all learning prompted by tutor)

---

[2] This intervention has also been applied with similar effect across a number of other disciplines using slightly different formats.

3.4 Beyond social constructivism

Thus far we have only discussed social constructivism in relation to pre-assessment activities and to students. However, we believe that social constructivism should apply to every stage of the assessment process and should actively engage both students and staff. We therefore propose a new model of sharing assessment standards which we call the 'cultivated community of practice' model.

3.4.1 Background

In recent years, a number of researchers have emphasised the importance of communities in the learning process. For example, Lave and Wenger (1991) argue that deep learning occurs as and when people come together in various contexts (educational establishments, the workplace, family settings) for various purposes. These groupings are defined by social relationships and the shared practices and understandings that come from mutual engagement in a common endeavour underpinned by a shared repertoire of resources. Lave and Wenger dub these groupings 'communities of practice'. Northedge (2003) similarly argues for the importance of knowledge communities in learning by emphasising learning's socio-cultural nature and the significance of shared language within communities. According to Northedge (2003, p.17), learning involves 'acquiring the capacity to participate in the discourses of an unfamiliar knowledge community, and teaching as supporting that participation'.

Our assessment intervention research (outlined in section 3.3 above) indicates the importance of the active engagement of students and staff in the assessment process, a shared assessment discourse and sense of shared endeavour. We therefore feel much affinity with researchers who take a step further and advocate a community of practice approach to learning as a whole. Yet, despite the appeal of this notion, it is unclear how such communities can be initiated and encouraged to grow.[3] In the context of higher education, Wenger (1998) makes the point that institutions fail to cultivate the requisite learning communities if learning within HE is considered something isolated and separate from

---

[3] The issue of how to cultivate communities of practice is further discussed in Chapter 7.

the learner's other activities, and stemming from an explicit and bounded teaching process. A belief that learning is an individual endeavour and not a community activity still lingers in some contexts. Indeed, previous research (e.g. Parker 2002) points in the UK to a critical lack of student engagement with academic communities. It seems that many students start university with little idea of what their course is either for or about and remain unenlightened into their second and third years.

How, then, can we buck the trend and engage students more fully in the learning process? Gibbs et al. (2004) suggest that students need to lose the passive role of 'the instructed' within processes controlled by academic experts and instead become interactive partners within a learning community. This seems to us to be the key and, in our cultivated community of practice model, we aim to move beyond a social constructivist approach in which expert tutors create formalised, active learning processes in order to guide novice students in learning the assessment standards of a module, to focussing on how students and tutors feed into and become part of the assessment practice of their particular disciplinary community. In order for students to fully understand the assessment standards within their discipline, they must participate in assessment processes in which the density of interactions and dialogue both between students and their peers as well as their tutors, formal and informal, is both valued and enhanced. Participants in such a community of practice will come to know both the explicit and tacit knowledge that the community holds, and peripheral (or new) participants are able to practise with and imitate more seasoned participants, thus becoming more fully and actively engaged within the community themselves.

3.4.2 The cultivated community of practice model (matrix quadrant 4)

What, then, does our cultivated community of practice model look like? First, there are two essential prerequisites which must be in place before the model can get off the ground (Rust et al. 2005):

- The course to be assessed must be constructively aligned (Biggs, 1999, p.1). This means that all aspects of the curriculum (learning outcomes, teaching and learning methods, assessment methods) must be clearly interrelated and logically consistent. This therefore suggests that an essential element of any constructively aligned course is a reasonable attempt to identify clear learning outcomes.

- There must be publicly stated assessment criteria which relate to the learning outcomes for the course. The criterion-referenced grid that we created for use by students and staff across the Business School at Oxford Brookes University (discussed in section 3.2 above) is an attempt at setting out 'clearly defined and explicit assessment criteria'. We came to understand, however, that the grid alone could not foster greater understanding among students nor create common standards among tutors, unless both actively engaged with the stated criteria—hence the need for a different kind of (non-explicit) model.

Once these two essential prerequisites are in place, both students and tutors can engage with the assessment criteria. We know from section 3.3 above that a pre-assessment workshop in which students actively apply the standards and criteria enables them to engage with those standards and criteria and results in improved performance. For tutors, research has shown that initial discussion with peers about the meaning of criteria, further discussion once some marking has been undertaken, and moderation after all marking has been completed leads, gradually, to increased common understanding and better standardisation of marking (Saunders and Davis 1998). For both students and staff, active engagement is the key to greater understanding.

In addition to engaging with the assessment criteria, students must engage with the feedback that they receive since, clearly, understanding and acting on feedback plays an important part in affecting future learning and achievement, and understanding of assessment (although research has shown that students often fail to find feedback useful, often fail to understand it, and may not even read it (Price et al. 2007, p.144)). There are, we suggest, a number of ways to engage students with feedback (see Rust et al. 2005, pp.234-5) including: two-stage assignments involving the students redrafting in the light of either tutor or peer feedback; running a seminar or workshop activity after an assignment has finally been summatively marked, which encourages students to derive conclusions about what to do differently in the future; giving only generic feedback on the class performance as a whole, thus allowing feedback to be given quickly and encouraging students to identify which bits of the feedback apply to them and therefore what they need to improve on next time.[4]

It is also worth pointing out that student engagement could be engineered to take place at almost any point in the assessment process, and is not only restricted to assessment criteria and feedback. Thus, students could actively engage during the creation of the work for assessment through, for example, self-assessment, or peer assessment, or both.

Having laid the groundwork, we can now move on to look at the structure of the cultivated community of practice model. As outlined in the Introduction to this chapter, our model of assessment involves two parallel cycles: one for students and one for staff. These two cycles are depicted below. It can be seen that the student cycle involves statement of explicit criteria, followed by active engagement with those criteria (e.g. at a pre-assessment marking workshop), followed by completion and submission of work to be assessed, followed by active engagement with the feedback on that work. We can therefore see that the cultivated community of practice model applies to all stages of assessment as experienced by the student—and the model suggests that, ultimately, community involvement will entail the student playing an active role in the construction and selection of criteria.

The staff cycle commences with alignment of the learning outcomes, the design of the assessment and the identification of criteria. This leads to tutors discussing the criteria with each other and with the assessment team (in order to brief students). This is followed by guidance being given to staff in order to facilitate consistent marking between individual markers, moderation according to the criteria, and provision of feedback.

---

[4] See Chapter 6 of this book, which gives a detailed analysis of feedback.

We can therefore see that the cultivated community of practice model applies to all stages of assessment as experienced by the tutor. (It is worth noting that the staff cycle is an oversimplification: the diagram below suggests that staff start the cycle from scratch when, in reality, they start the cycle within a pre-existing, dynamic process.)

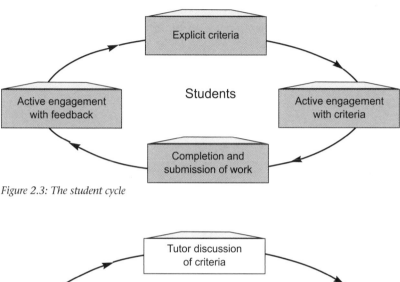

Figure 2.3: The student cycle

Figure 2.4: The staff cycle

What sets our cultivated community of practice model apart from social constructivist models—and what moves the cultivated community of practice model from quadrant 3 of the matrix (where social constructivist models sit) to quadrant 4 of the matrix (see section 2)—is that the student and the staff cycles, rather than being separate, make up the two halves of one dynamic system. *It is only when you move from two distinct cycles to two interacting cycles that you have entered quadrant 4.*

Each cycle informs the other, thus a common understanding of assessment based on a shared discourse is constantly evolving between students and staff within a dynamic community of practice. Ideally, we believe that each cycle should inform the other at every stage, but with an eye on practicality, the cycles must engage with one another at least twice, we believe. First, at the stage of initial engagement with the criteria, the emerging common understanding of the tutors must inform the way in which the assessment criteria are written as well as the pre-assessment workshop conducted with the students. Likewise, any issues (e.g. of misinterpretation of criteria or how they might relate to the assessment task) raised by the students at the workshop must be fed back and further engaged with by the tutors. (Note that a workshop would not be conducted in every cycle, rather just once or twice during a programme.) Second, once the work has been marked, the quality of the

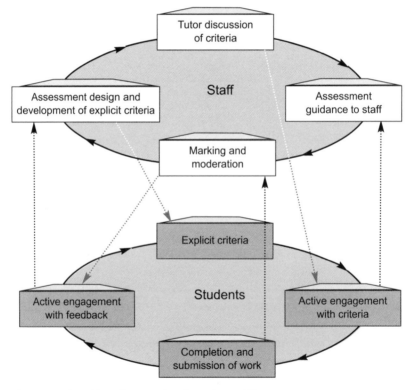

Figure 2.5: The cultivated community of practice model[5]

[5] This figure is reproduced from Rust, O'Donovan and Price 2005.

work, the students' comments on the work and the marking, and the quality of the tutor feedback should be fed back and further engaged with by the tutors (probably as part of the tutors' initial engagement with the criteria at the start of the next cycle).

We can therefore see that the cultivated community of practice model of assessment:

(1) applies to every stage of the assessment process and

(2) actively engages both students and staff.

As outlined in section 2, it is important to recognise that the cultivated community of practice model does not mark a departure from all previous models of sharing assessment standards. Rather, it can be seen as a logical progression on from previous models. It retains those features of previous models that are most relevant or apt in today's HE environment of ever-increasing class sizes and ever-decreasing student–staff contact time, while discarding those features that are no longer relevant or fail to work. Thus, like the explicit model, the cultivated community of practice model commences with the premise that there must be publicly stated assessment criteria for all courses. Without this kind of clarity, it is not possible for students (or staff) to begin to engage with the criteria. However, the model acknowledges that clarity alone is not sufficient. Like the traditional model, it highlights the importance of tacit knowledge—in addition to explicit knowledge, there exists an underlying body of tacit knowledge (comprising, for example, context and previous experiences) which does not lend itself to explicit articulation and which cannot be precisely defined. The cultivated community of practice model also (like the social constructivist approach) recognises that, in order for students to absorb this tacit knowledge, they must actively engage in tasks that involve them in using and applying the standards and criteria. Knowledge comes through use in this context. However, the model finally takes one step further on from the social constructivist approach. It proposes that in order to come to a full understanding of assessment standards over time, students must become engaged not only with specific tasks set by expert tutors, but also within a broad and rich community of academic practice and this, in turn, enables them to generate and lead their own activities aimed at enhancing their understanding of assessment standards. For example, self-generated learning groups in which students meet informally to discuss and comment on their own and others' work is a student-led practice which supports and consolidates understanding over time and outside the formal, classroom environment. A rich community of practice should enable students to interact with one another and with their tutors on many interrelated levels. It should enable practices and a shared discourse to be absorbed over time. It should provide the opportunity for more experienced students to induct their less experienced peers into the practices of the community. In this way, the traditional labels of 'instructed' and 'instructor' are diluted, and students and tutors become partners in the collaborative venture of learning— although, of course, tutors remain the 'final' assessors.

There is, however, one caveat that we should highlight in relation to the cultivated community of practice model—it is more speculative than the other models that we have discussed in this chapter. It is a model of how we believe assessment standards should be shared among staff and students and, in principle, has much to recommend it, but in practice we have no robust causal evidence that it works within the specific context of assessment. Although in Chapter 7 of this book we do discuss robust research that evidences the positive association of 'community', in terms of enhanced student interaction with peers and tutors, and academic performance and personal growth (Astin 1984, 1993). However, there is no specific road map that is assured of success on how to seed or initiate a community of practice. Communities of practice are nudged and guided into fruition rather than being deliberately and formally seeded. Communities evolve gradually, over time, taking on life and momentum of their own, developing in particular directions according to the needs and desires of their members and whilst their development can be shepherded they may resist formalised initiation (Wenger et al. 2002).[6] They can of course also break down over time. We might speculate that some disciplines, such as fine art or drama, exhibit features of a community of practice in which learning is driven by interaction, imitation and engagement with the disciplinary community, but this is only speculation.

[6] Although some might argue that Alverno College in the US (see Chapter 1, section 2.6) is possibly an example of a community of practice that has been deliberately seeded.

The Cultivated Community of Practice Model

Key features

- Retains and relies on characteristics from previous models
- Sees tacit knowledge as key
- Embraces active learning
- Proposes a 'community of practice' in which students & staff are joint partners

Disadvantages

- Lack of causal evidence

4. Conclusion

This chapter has illustrated that an understanding of assessment standards is a vital foundation for the development of broader assessment literacy. Specifically, the chapter has:

- detailed our own theoretical approach to the sharing of assessment standards (the matrix and the cultivated community of practice model);
- outlined the history of theoretical approaches to the sharing of assessment standards (via the traditional, explicit and social constructivist models); and
- indicated how our own approach relates to these historical models, which features of these models it retains, and why.

Now that the theory has been clearly set out, the next step is to explain how that theory works in practice. How can a cultivated community of practice approach ensure greater understanding of assessment standards and criteria amongst today's students? What concrete steps can we take to secure better performance across the student body? The following chapters explore these kinds of questions, and suggest practical and research-tested solutions to them.

Planning Assessment

1. Introduction

In Chapter 2, we discussed our theoretical approach to assessment, and set out in detail our cultivated community of practice model of the sharing of assessment standards. Over the next four chapters we will concentrate on the practicalities of actually carrying out assessment. The process of assessment can be split into four stages (hence the four chapters):

- planning assessment (with a focus on planning at programme level)
- pre-assessment activity (for students)
- assessment activity (looking at assessment tasks and marking), and
- post-assessment activity (feedback).

This chapter concentrates on the planning of assessment. We begin by sketching out, and highlighting the failings of, the current, often module-focused, approach to planning assessment in the UK, which leads into a discussion of the benefits of taking a programme-wide approach to designing assessment (see also Chapter 1, section 2.6). We then turn our attention to the kinds of decisions that need to made when starting to plan a programme-level assessment strategy, and we conclude with a summary of the concrete approaches to programme-level assessment that are already in use in some institutions.

2. Context: the current state of assessment design in higher education in the UK

Planning and implementation of programmes within higher education are usually focused on content and delivery rather than assessment. The design processes of these programmes take place within a much wider context and, naturally, are constrained by certain aspects of that wider context—institutional missions and systems, for example, or the nature of overall course design. However, the planning of assessment at programme level is sometimes an afterthought or even largely ignored.

We recommend that assessment design should be undertaken by the programme or course leader(s) in conjunction with their programme/course teams. The aim is to devise a comprehensive and robust assessment strategy that can ensure the learning outcomes of the programme have been met, distinguish between the performance of individual students, and improve student learning. Typically, however, the planning of assessment in the UK is fragmented, and carried out at the level of individual modules (with aggregation of marks at this level being used speciously to determine ultimate degree classifications). Any systematic or integrated approach to assessment at programme level (or indeed cross-programmes) has largely been absent from modularised programmes or, with the exception of some programmes such as art and design, nominally attributed to a dissertation or extended essay. This lack is of particular importance since, without such integration, synthesis is largely left up to the student and not assessed.

This focus on the module (or micro) level has a number of undesirable consequences. For example, although the module outcomes are assessed, it does not thereby mean that the outcomes of the overall programme are assessed. A student may have completed all the module assessments satisfactorily, but it does not necessarily follow that s/he has met the essential requirements at programme level, even if an attempt has been made to map module outcomes to those of the programme. In other words, there needs to be some kind of *synthesis* of the module outcomes in order for us to be able to say that a student has successfully achieved the programme outcomes. A lack of synthesis encourages a 'banking' approach to learning where students' main aim is that of attaining the requisite grades or marks to pass the module (and so programme). There is little time within modules to support the development of assessment literacy, or to focus on formative assessment, or for staff to provide meaningful feedback on slowly-learnt academic literacies (the skill of critical thinking, for example) or more complex learning. These kinds of higher-order skills and learning are difficult to assess at module level and take time to develop. Assigning a summative mark in a module situated early in a programme may disadvantage students whose understandings grow throughout the programme. In addition, the modular structure is by definition fragmentary, which makes it problematic for students and staff alike to comprehend either the links between the modules or the coherence of the programme as a whole. And finally, assessment at module level involves what Rust (2007, 2011) has referred to as 'questionable statistical practices', including the custom of aggregating outcomes judged against different criteria into a single mark, thus obscuring the progress and attainment of students against each programme outcome.[1,2]

These kinds of deficiencies have prompted recent calls for a broader, more comprehensive approach to assessment focusing on the programme rather than the module level. Researchers have contended that a programme-wide approach to assessment would have a number of wide-ranging benefits, including financial advantage (Knight 2000), student retention (Yorke 2001a, 2001b), lifelong learning and employability (Boud 2000; Boud and Falchikov 2006; Knight and Yorke 2003; Yorke and Knight 2006), and improved student learning (Rust 2002; Havnes 2007, 2008). As yet, however, the literature contains little concrete advice relating to the design of programme-level assessment.

---

[1] Although some modular programmes incorporate 'capstone modules', which assess students towards the end of a year and/or programme, the marks from these modules are often aggregated with other module marks, hence do not provide an adequate solution to these issues. (See section 5.2 for more detail on capstone modules.)

[2] See Rust (2007, 2011) for more detail on these practices.

3. Programme-level assessment: the way forward

We suggest that assessment only at the module level is far from ideal. An adequate assessment strategy should measure the achievement of programme outcomes, take into account slowly-learnt literacies and complex learning, and provide a clear picture of what it is to be a graduate. The solution would seem to be to focus at the programme rather than the module level and to design an assessment strategy that is coherent, integrated across the whole period of study of the programme, and thus capable of tracking the development of slowly-learnt literacies and higher-order learning over time. This is not easily or quickly done, though, largely because of a lack of precedent and because of the now deeply engrained modular approach. Furthermore, the time currently allocated to review and validation processes within institutions is not great enough to consider whether programme outcomes are being delivered at module level, hence this aspect of validation is sometimes nothing more than a tick box exercise.

4. The elements of a programme-level assessment strategy

In this section we examine the kinds of factors that need to be considered, and the decisions that need to be made, in planning a programme-level assessment strategy. This is not an exhaustive list, but rather a broad indication of decisions relevant to programme-level planning. Some of these decisions will depend on the nature of the discipline being assessed, while others will be guided by preference or utility. It is important to bear in mind, however, that all of these decisions will be to some extent contextual—a matter of emphasis rather than of absolutes—and that they will be interrelated and synchronous, rather than being made sequentially.

It is also important to note that the overall institutional context will act as a constraint on programme design and the development of assessment strategies at programme level (and is likely to be considered in validation and other quality assurance procedures). Different institutions have different missions or strengths—such as employability; particular graduate attributes; education for the professions; research led programmes; a focus on lifelong learning, etc.—and these differences in emphasis will, naturally, inform programme and assessment design.

And finally the assessment of programme outcomes will, of course, have to be valid. In order to make a valid assessment it is first of all necessary to decide what is being assessing—what it is that makes a graduate of history a historian, for example. Then it is necessary to consider how that can be assessed—using what kinds of tasks. And finally we must consider how marks can be allocated to those tasks such that we are adequately assessing whether or not someone has made the grade of 'historian'.

4.1 Decision point 1: integration or mapping

The first decision lies in whether the assessment of the programme is to be achieved through either (a) integrated assessment which directly assesses the programme outcomes, or (b) coherent assessment of constituent elements of programme outcomes, i.e. assessing unit level outcomes and relying on coherent mapping to ensure the indirect assessment of the programme outcomes, or (c) an intentional combination of these two methods. This decision will be determined at the appropriate level by the nature of the programme outcomes and discipline(s) involved. For instance, a doctor's diagnostic ability rests on the ability to integrate multiple knowledge areas. As a result, the assessment of a doctor's diagnostic skill as both valid and reliable requires that this integration or synthesis be assessed. So, being able to name every bone in the body should not compensate for poor diagnostic skills. In contrast, we are aware of a programme in the History of Art in which all the modules were designed with similar learning outcomes (essentially programme outcomes), the difference being that each module focussed on a different period of Art History.

Clearly, as we noted right back in the first paragraph of section 2, there will be a number of constraints in the wider context that will limit the choice between (a), (b), or (c). These constraints are often at the institutional level so, for example, if our institution operates a modular system across the board, choice (a) will be a considerable challenge.

4.2 Decision point 2: allocation of resources

This brings us to the second decision, which involves allocation of resources. There are two strands to this decision point:

Decision point 2(a)

This strand centres on the inevitable trade-off between the construct validity, reliability, and manageability of assessment at both programme and task level, which means that we need to decide, for a task or for particular elements of a programme, which of these three factors is/are the more important—and, in an environment of limited resources, which we will allocate more resource to. To return to our medical example—it is imperative that doctors are able to diagnose accurately and to make correct healthcare decisions, and the public needs to be assured of this. We would therefore hope that medical science programmes assess their students with high validity and high reliability at the expense of manageability (i.e. despite the fact that this type of assessment is time-consuming and expensive). In other words, we judge that when assessing doctors we should direct a high level of resource towards ensuring (with maximum validity and reliability) that they really do know their subject and can apply it. However, in other disciplines which do not deal in matters of life and death, it may be more appropriate to develop an assessment regime that is valid and manageable, but less reliable. So, for example, it may be harder or more challenging to assess 'design' with high reliability. And it may be less imperative that we assess 'design' with high reliability. We may therefore be wise to direct the majority of our resource towards ensuring valid and manageable assessment in this case, while accepting that, since reliable assessment is more difficult (and arguably less important), it does not merit a high allocation of resource. Stobart (2008, p.110) demonstrates this trade-off well with the visual image of a 'one-handed clock', where the position of the one hand between the three points on the clock face of validity, reliability and manageability indicates that high validity and reliability may come at the cost of manageability, while high validity and manageability may come at the cost of reliability.

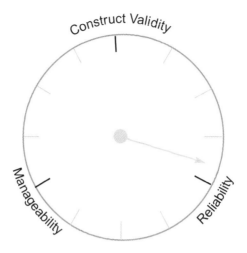

Figure 3.1: Stobart's one-handed clock [3]

Decision point 2(b)

This decision point centres on issues of resource allocation other than those thrown up by the validity/reliability/manageability equation described above. Again, in an environment of limited means, we need to make decisions about where we should concentrate the limited resources available to us.

For example, we may judge that different years of a degree programme merit different kinds of assessment and so different kinds of resource allocation. We may, perhaps, wish to concentrate our resources in the second and third years, with the majority of assessments taking place at these points once students have become competent practitioners in their subjects and are ready to have their knowledge and skills assessed.

The matter of resource allocation is more complicated than this, however. It may be, for example, that formative assessment is most appropriate during the first year when students are being inducted into academic life and practice and so require guidance, constructive feedback and multiple opportunities to practise new skills. This kind

---

[3] This diagram appears in Stobart, 2008, p.110 and is reproduced with kind permission of the publisher, Routledge.

of assessment may be relatively resource-light in terms of formal administration, but resource-heavy in terms of the staff time spent on giving detailed feedback, commenting on drafts, meeting with students, etc. Summative assessment—possibly more appropriate at later years in the programme—may be more costly (involving payment of external examiners and invigilators, compilation and printing of exam papers, etc.). Decisions about resources involve not only choices about where to direct resource but also choices about which kind of resource is most appropriate for a given task or situation.

In a similar vein, some types of skill or knowledge may lend themselves better to a particular type of assessment. Thus slowly-learnt literacies lend themselves best to formative assessment. It is only through repeated practice and feedback over the long term that a student will fully grasp the skill of critical analysis, for example. It may be that slowly-learnt literacies are confirmed via summative assessment, but summative assessment does not directly assess slowly-learnt literacies. Since such slowly-learnt literacies are often fundamental to learning, we may choose to direct a high level of resource (in the form of formative assessment) towards them throughout the course of the programme. Or we may, as Knight (2000) suggests, focus on giving useful and swift formative feedback for such slowly-learnt literacies, thereby supporting students in developing their own learning in these areas over the duration of their programme and so freeing up more staff time.

Student retention is yet another area that is linked with resource allocation. As Yorke (2003) points out, retention is beneficial for the institution as well as for the student, since non-completion is detrimental to institutional income. We may therefore choose to direct resource towards strategies that are known to result in higher levels of retention (plenty of formative assessment in the first year for example, with summative assessment being delayed until later years) with the aim of increasing financial resource for the institution as a whole.

4.3 Decision point 3: formative and summative assessment

This brings us to our third decision about the balance between formative and summative assessment, both across a programme and within a module. While it may be fashionable to simplify and revere formative assessment, the issues surrounding employing an appropriate balance between summative and formative are complex and contextual, leading us to consider a number of interdependent tensions:[4]

(a) Student time in balancing summative and formative assessment

A HEPI study (Sastry and Bekhradnia 2007) indicated that students need to spend approximately 30 hours per week studying in order to achieve the learning outcomes set for full-time higher education. Yet on average they were found to spend less (and sometimes considerably less) time studying than this. Summative assessment has been used in many institutions to ensure that students spend adequate time on the task in hand, but this can result in students adopting strategic approaches to their learning (Gibbs and Dunbar-Goddet 2007), as well as leading to concerns about the over-assessment of students. But if we reduce the quantity of summative assessment in favour of formative assessment in an attempt to address such concerns, we may well find that some students devote even less time to their studies.

(b) Staff time in balancing summative and formative assessment

Summative assessments have often been considered more resource-intensive than formative because of the administrative work required to verify and record results. Yet, as we saw in section 4.2 above, summative assessment (by definition) does not involve the highly resource-intensive activity of providing rich formative feedback. It is therefore not obvious that one type of assessment is more time-consuming than the other, and it is correspondingly unclear how a change in the balance between summative and formative assessment might impact on staff time.

---

[4] See 'Assessment—an ASKe position paper' (available at: http://www.brookes.ac.uk/aske/Perspectives/positionpaper.html) for more detail on these issues; also Price, Carroll at al. 2010.

(c) Student engagement in balancing summative and formative assessment

Teaching staff are aware that, more often than not, students need to be encouraged to engage with learning activities—and this encouragement often takes the form of marks. Thus many formative assessment tasks will be allocated a proportion of the summative marks in order to ensure that students actually do the work—and this changes the nature of the assessment for all parties involved. But it is difficult to see how one can devise systems of monitoring participation that do not conflate summative and formative assessment in this way—particularly in mass higher education systems where students find it easy to remain anonymous.

(d) High-stakes assessment in balancing summative and formative assessment

As the amount of summative assessment reduces, so the assessment stakes are raised. Less assessment means more high-stakes assessment. Many students find high-stakes assessment stressful and such assessment, by definition, is very likely to have a negative impact on progression rates, since any underperformance has higher impact. Furthermore, high-stakes assessment leaves fewer opportunities for those students who need to 'recover' their position (i.e. make up for poor performance in one or more assessed tasks). And it offers little flexibility in meeting the needs of a diverse student body. For all students, high-stakes assessment must be supported by appropriate preparation in terms of practice, formative feedback and time (Yorke 2003).

(e) Feedback in balancing summative and formative assessment

When feedback is provided on work that combines formative and summative assessment, students may perceive the feedback to be more a justification of the grade awarded than advice about how to improve the work, despite markers' best intentions (Handley et al. 2008). This negative perception from students naturally undermines the purpose of formative assessment.[5]

---

[5] See section 5.3.1 in Chapter 6 of this book for more discussion on this issue.

(f) Accrediting learning in balancing summative and formative assessment

Summative assessment measures achievement of learning outcomes. The fairest and most important point for that measurement, then, is surely at the end of a programme when, we assume, students are able to demonstrate their highest level of learning (given sufficient time to prepare). The Burgess Report (2007) considered many inadequacies with current degree classification systems, including the fact that one final classification signifier (2.1, Third, etc.) inadequately reflects the range of achievements of students within and between classifications. In a modular programme, credits are 'collected' along the way, sometimes in a range of areas/subjects/disciplines. All collected credits contribute to the learning outcomes of the programme, but measurement may take place well before the end of the programme and a final overall mark is calculated from different parts of the programme. Interestingly, there is evidence (Rust 2001) to suggest that far fewer summative marks are required (six in one study) than are currently generated to 'accurately' calculate final degree classification. However, if we are accrediting achievement of learning outcomes in named degrees we need to be assured that the qualification awarded reflects the achievement of the programme learning outcomes as a whole. Often, this is not the same as the sum of the component parts. It may be that summative assessment towards the end of the programme based on programme outcomes can provide a more accurate reflection of student achievement, thereby allowing formative assessment to support learning.

Summary of decision point 3

We can see, then, that there are considerable issues surrounding the question of what might constitute an appropriate balance between summative and formative assessment, and it is not immediately obvious how we can pose a simple, satisfactory and sustainable solution. In many universities the distinction between formative and summative has become blurred, with assessment tasks serving dual roles. Yet, as Sadler (1989, p.20) points out, there is an essential difference between the two: 'Summative contrasts with formative assessment in that it is concerned with summing up or summarising the achievement status of a student, and it is geared towards reporting at the end of a course of study especially for purposes of certification. It is essentially passive and does not normally have immediate impact on learning.'

Having a clear understanding of the difference between formative and summative assessment is an important part of assessment literacy. If, as Sadler suggests, summative and formative assessment are essentially incompatible, and if, as the previous paragraphs imply, summative assessment largely eliminates the significant benefits of formative, then the dominance of summative results is probably what lies behind cries of over-assessment. If, on the other hand, assessment is for learning, then over-assessment is a meaningless idea—as long as assessment tasks are calculated as an integral part of allocated study hours. Changing the balance between formative and summative would require significant changes in other areas in order to support current student study habits.

An emphasis on integrated assessment will have an effect on other factors such as the timing of summative assessment—it is likely to be more appropriate to assess integrated knowledge, slowly learnt skills and key concepts later in a programme. Integrated assessment is also likely to diminish the diversity of assessment and, interestingly, it has been shown that the more diverse the assessment tasks, the less well students perform (Gibbs and Dunbar-Goddet 2007). However, while a reduction in diversity may be appropriate in those disciplines requiring constant practice of particular skills (diagnostics in medicine, for example), it may prove more problematic in multidisciplinary areas such as business. We discuss these issues further in the following section.

4.4 Decision point 4: nature of assessment task

The final decision to be made when planning assessment at programme level relates to the nature of the assessment tasks set. More specifically, the variety and the challenge of the assessment tasks set.

It is well known that within a modular system some students actively choose modules to avoid or to secure particular types of assessment— those who dislike exams may favour modules that are coursework dominated, or those who prefer to expend little effort may favour modules with a high level of group work, for example. By adopting this tactic, these students tend to expose themselves to a limited range of assessment types and may actively choose modules that fit poorly with their long-term goals and aspirations, thereby decreasing the coherence of their overall programmes. Yet it is generally considered that a wide variety of assessment types is beneficial in terms of inclusivity, fairness and motivation. There is a danger, however, of having too great a variety of assessment within a programme since, in order to fully understand and become proficient with a particular assessment technique, students need the opportunity to practise that technique. They need, in other words, to encounter a particular type of assessment task more than once, and ideally several times.

The key is to achieve a suitable balance between the variety and challenge of assessment, such that students become proficient with a variety of techniques yet are still stretched by the summative assessments that they encounter. Clearly, within a programme-level approach, it should be possible gradually to introduce a number of assessment techniques across the programme so that students encounter some variety. Repeated formative assessments will provide the practice that students need in order to become familiar with a particular type of assessment. The question then becomes how, when it comes to the final summative assessment, can we test that students have really understood the task and are not just replicating what they have learnt during the practice sessions? One answer might be to employ similar scenarios or contexts when practising a particular type of assessment, but then to introduce an entirely new scenario or context when it comes to a summative assessment of the same type. For example, in the case of Business Studies, you might introduce a different industry context for the summative assessment. This approach has the advantage that students should already be familiar with the assessment task used but will need to apply thought and reasoning when adapting that task to the new context, thereby confirming whether or not they have really understood the task at hand.

5. Approaches to designing programme-level assessment

As we have seen in the preceding sections, a number of decisions need to be made before we are in a position to move on and implement a particular programme-level assessment design. Clearly, the next step of incorporating programme assessment into modular or unitised programmes in reality is not an easy one, but there are at least four different routes that can be taken and are currently used (or under development) in institutions in Europe, the US and Australia.

5.1 Accumulative integrative project

This approach requires a long, compulsory core module, running for say a year, and involving an integrative 'project', or case study. This is supported by a number of (probably) shorter (and some possibly elective) modules running alongside, which contribute to the project by providing the appropriate knowledge and skills. When rendered diagrammatically, this approach is sometimes called the buttressed building model. On an automotive engineering course, for example, the project might be to build a car. The supporting modules might focus on different topics such as materials science, systems engineering, etc. (see below).

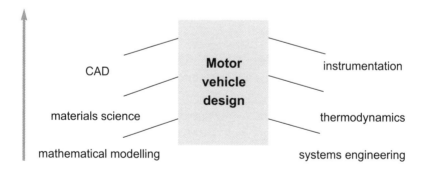

Figure 3.2: The buttressed building model in relation to automotive engineering [6]

---

[6] This diagram is reproduced from Baume and Baume, 1992, p.10 with kind permission of the authors.

5.2 Summative integrative project and/or assessment period

Rather than running throughout the course, like a spine, as in the previous example, this approach designs the integrative assessment to come towards the end—of a year, and/or the programme as a whole. The most common example of this occurs in the US in the form of the 'capstone module', although such modules are becoming increasingly common in the UK and Australia as well. The Office of Assessment and Accreditation at Indiana State University describes a capstone course as 'a course in which students undergo a cumulative experience—the purpose of the course is to apply what has been learned in a course or to engage in an experience that summarizes what has been learned as a result of successful enrolment in a program... Capstone courses take many forms—seminars, required internship/field experiences, application courses, etc.'[7] In the UK, dissertations have typically been used to assess the culmination of academic skills and abilities, despite their tendency to narrow the scope of study rather than requiring integration across the full range of study.

Some UK universities have an academic year comprising two teaching terms followed by a shorter assessment term, the majority of which is examination based, with examinations linked to individual courses taken. There is no reason, however, why integrative examinations could not be set—and more imaginative and authentic assessments (rather than just exams) used.

In the Business School at Maastricht University in the Netherlands, for example, there is an integrative assessment period at the end of each term. A term comprises an eight week teaching block followed by four weeks during which the students are put into groups and undertake an integrative project based on what they have learnt that term.

5.3 Integrative assessment task

The Business School at Coventry University is currently (in 2011) designing a slightly different approach again, whereby an integrative

---

[7] See http://assessment.aas.duke.edu/documents/
Capstone_Assessment_Introduction.ppt.

assessment task will be used in each year to assess the outcomes of a group of three modules.

The aim is that for each year of Coventry's Business Management programmes there will be a unifying theme that focuses on a different sector as exemplified by a local employer. The employer will either be a global brand or have global reach. In the second semester of each year assessment will take place via a large integrative task that will be designed to assess the learning from the three modules. The three first year modules will cover the following areas: foundations of management, quantitative skills for management, and basic management affairs. The current idea (under development at the time of writing) is that although there will only be one major assessment product for the three modules, this product may be assessed separately for each module using different criteria appropriate to each module's different learning outcomes.

This approach has been driven in large part by Coventry's policy that more assessment should be integrative. It also provides an opportunity for students to tackle a larger, more complex and real-world assessment task.

5.4 Assessment blocks

A radical new idea that has been developed at Brunel University through a change in their regulations (and taken up by four degree programmes so far) is to allow the separation of what have been called 'study blocks' from 'assessment blocks'. Thus assessment blocks (which include synoptic examinations at every level of the course) focus on the integration of both specific and general course outcomes, and are specified separately from formal teaching, or study blocks. In this way, assessment blocks can relate to a number of study blocks, but there is also room for conventional modules where the study and assessment blocks completely coincide.

The revisions to the programmes at Brunel have resulted in a major reduction in assessment, and staff time has therefore been shifted to provide more contact with students and more student support, as well as an increased focus on formative assessment. It is hoped that students' critical thinking and analysis skills will improve as a result. [8]

5.5 Portfolio

The portfolio is similar to the accumulative integrative project in that it runs like a spine throughout the course. In this case, students evaluate their own work and make decisions about which pieces should be included in their portfolios. A portfolio is therefore a selection, rather than simply an accumulated collection, of work. In a growing number of cases, the portfolio is no longer physical, but electronic. In the UK, personal development planning has often been used in conjunction with portfolios, and some institutions have actually included this as a long, thin module within the curriculum.

The collection of work in a portfolio is not in itself integrative, but periodic reflection on what has been learnt, the identification of strengths and weaknesses, and the selection and use of evidence from the portfolio certainly can be. Rose Hulman Institute of Technology in the US utilises the helpful idea of 'my best example yet', requiring students to regularly reflect on, and update, their electronic portfolios.

6. Conclusion

In this chapter, we have explored the activity of planning assessment. We have seen that, in the UK in particular, the planning of assessment is focussed on the module or micro level, which leads to a number of negative consequences including few opportunities for provision of formative feedback, and a related lack of recognition for the kind of high-level, complex learning that develops slowly over time. This situation has led to calls for a more comprehensive approach to assessment design that focuses on planning at the programme or macro level.

We argue that, when planning programme-level assessment, certain decisions need to be made as part of the development of a particular assessment strategy. These decisions cover issues such as how the assessment of the programme is to be achieved; where limited resources

[8]   See http://www.pass.brad.ac.uk/ for more information on this approach.

should be directed; the interrelation and balance between summative and formative assessment; and the nature of assessment tasks.

We conclude that there exist a number of possible approaches to designing programme-level assessment. Although these are not yet commonly used in the UK, they do provide a starting point for planning at the macro level and we can of course expect that, as programme-level assessment strategies become more widespread within the UK, there will be a corresponding growth in concrete examples and practices on which assessment design teams (and all other interested parties) can draw.

Pre-Assessment Activity

1. Introduction

In the previous chapter, we looked at planning assessment, emphasising the benefits of taking a programme-wide approach to assessment design and summarising some of the extant programme-level approaches. We are now in a position to move on to the next stage in the assessment process—pre-assessment activity with/for students. This chapter therefore examines the kinds of techniques and exercises that can be used to prepare students for assessment, to increase their assessment literacy, and to improve their learning. We focus especially on our own significant and widely adopted assessment intervention, which improves student learning by developing student understanding of assessment criteria and processes by means of a marking exercise and workshop discussion.

1.1 What is pre-assessment activity?

By 'pre-assessment activity' we mean the kinds of exercises or activities in which tutors can engage their students (prior to them undertaking assessed tasks) in order to increase student understanding of the nature of assessment, the criteria and standards, and the assessment processes that will be used to assess their work, thus enabling them to see the point of the task and perform more ably at an earlier stage. In other words, this chapter explores ways in which we can enhance student assessment literacy early on via structured activities that are known to enhance understanding of the assessment process in general and, in particular, of the rules and rationales that staff apply and provide when marking students' work. In terms of the definition of assessment literacy that we set out in Chapter 1, this practice will enhance students' assessment literacy by improving their: conceptual understanding of assessment (the basic principles of valid assessment practice plus the terminology used); understanding of the nature, meaning and level of assessment criteria and standards; skills in self-assessment and peer review; and familiarity with technical approaches to assessment (i.e. skills, techniques and methods used together with their purpose and efficacy).

Enhancement of assessment literacy can occur at different levels. So, for example, Sadler (2010) talks about, as a starting point, one simple and task-focused pre-assessment activity which involves students looking at a very basic level at an assignment task and underlining all the verbs, then all the nouns that appear there, so that they are quite clear about what they need to do, to or with what in order to satisfy the assessment criteria. Examples of more sophisticated activities that can improve assessment literacy include discussion about assessment criteria, use of exemplars, exercises in applying marking criteria, peer review, and self-assessment exercises. These kinds of activities aim to help students understand the nature of assessment tasks, to understand how they should proceed when presented with specific assessment tasks—in essence, they encourage students to start thinking like assessors. Recent research by Kay Sambell illustrates how students can be guided towards developing 'assessor-like' thinking—as well as indicating what a struggle this shift in viewpoint can be for some students. In Sambell's 2010 study, Early Childhood Studies students were asked to prepare a short piece of writing in response to the task: 'Explain the social construction of childhood to a first year student.' These students then brought their work to a phased workshop. In phase 1 of the workshop, the students were asked to read, discuss and place in rank order four exemplar responses to the task above. (Exemplar 1 was the 'best' and represented a sound response to the question. Exemplar 2 was a reasonable but more limited response. Exemplar 3 was a fair attempt but included a lot of illustrative detail which required clearer introduction and explanation. Exemplar 4 entirely misunderstood the key concept. All four exemplars displayed errors of convention such as spelling, grammar and citation.) In phase 2, tutors revealed the ranking that they had given the exemplars, including explaining the reasoning behind their ranking. In phase 3, the students were asked to generate feedback for each exemplar and reflect on how they would change their own work in the light of the tutor dialogue. During phase 1, the students focused on surface features and on how to write, showing preoccupation with external conventions such as referencing. They ignored issues relating to the subject domain. Phase 2 revealed that students were unable to rank exemplars in the same order as tutors—they tended to either muddle the two best exemplars or prefer the worst exemplar and dislike the best. However, when the students re-examined the exemplars in the light of the tutor explanation, a few of them began to grasp the relevant assessment requirements and to explain them to their peers—but this transformation to thinking like an assessor proved to be a huge struggle for many, with many finding it difficult to move beyond superficial characteristics of grammar and spelling. This transformation of thought is crucial to assessment literacy and, as such, represents a threshold concept[1]—once one has grasped how to think like an assessor, one is able to move towards a deeper understanding and engagement. In the remainder of this chapter we look in detail at strategies that can be used to enhance students' assessment literacy and, in particular, to enable them to develop an assessor's understanding of assessment.

1.2 The problem of tacit knowledge

We noted earlier in this book that there has been increasing acknowledgement over recent years by the government, public and within higher education that there needs to be greater transparency and consistency with regard to assessment and, as a result, there has been a determined effort to make standards clearer to all stakeholders (staff, students, parents, employers). As discussed in Chapter 2 (section 3.2), this effort has focussed on making explicit statements with regard to all aspects of assessment, with particular emphasis on learning outcomes, level descriptors and disciplinary benchmarks. However, as we also saw in Chapter 2, no matter how explicit we (as teaching staff) are with regard to assessment processes, criteria and standards, it is still

---

[1] A concept which represents a transformed perspective or way of understanding something without which the learner cannot progress (Meyer & Land 2006).

not possible to convey everything that we know about assessment to our students or even each other. There still remains a gap between what we are able to articulate explicitly and the body of knowledge that we make use of in our day-to-day dealings with assessment. This gap relates specifically to tacit knowledge—issues of academic language, context, experience and expectation that cannot be articulated easily, if at all (we are probably not even aware that we 'know' some of these things!)—and the way that we gain this tacit knowledge is not through telling, but by drawing on our experience of being assessed in the past and also by being inducted into an academic community of practice in which we can observe academic and assessment processes in action, take note of examples, ask questions, and ultimately imitate and practise our new-found knowledge of those processes. The slippage from 'we' (us as teaching staff) to 'we' (us as learners) in the previous sentence is quite deliberate since it is not only students who need to be inducted into an academic community of practice. New members of staff (experienced staff who are new to an institution, as well as novices) also require inducting into the academic and assessment processes of the institution—they need to learn, via imitation and practice, that this is the way things are done 'around here'.

Since this gap exists between staff (who do possess the relevant tacit knowledge) and students (who do not) and since it is the role of staff to teach students and to aid them in closing knowledge gaps, it is vital that we find effective ways of passing our tacit knowledge of assessment practices, criteria and standards on to our students, thereby increasing their assessment literacy. And this is something that must be done before students undertake an assessment task since, in our view, the purpose of an assessment task is not student discovery of the standards and criteria of assessment, but is learning and achievement in the student's subject. This chapter therefore sets out some concrete ways in which this can be attempted.

1.3 The structure of this chapter

Early claims from the USA (Nelson 1994) and case studies from the UK (Forbes and Spence 1991; Hughes 1995) indicated that involving students in marking exercises and peer marking may result in a significant subsequent improvement in their work, suggesting that this would be a fruitful area for further investigation. More recently, a small number of empirical studies undertaken in the UK have developed this theme and illustrated that when students take part in activities such as marking exercises; discussions about assessment criteria and exemplars; and peer review and self-assessment, their understanding of the assessment criteria and standards is enhanced, along with their performance when undertaking future assessed tasks. In this chapter we examine some of these studies in detail, beginning with our own assessment intervention (already touched on in Chapter 2), which improves student learning by developing student understanding of assessment criteria and processes via a marking exercise and workshop discussion (Rust et al. 2003). Our intervention is by far the largest and most sustained of the studies that we discuss, with results replicated over three years and evidence that improved student performance continues beyond the end point of the intervention. As a result, our intervention has been widely adopted across the sector, both nationally and internationally.

We also look at research led by Paul Orsmond and Stephen Merry—a set of studies on a smaller scale exploring the use of student-constructed marking criteria in conjunction with exemplars, peer review and self-assessment (Orsmond et al. 2002, 2004). And we end with a very brief summary of other studies which use interventions to improve student understanding of assessment criteria.

We conclude that by using the kind of intervention techniques outlined in these studies, it is possible to improve students' learning, assessment literacy, and performance—and it is possible to do this even in today's HE climate of large classes, minimal student/staff contact time, and limited resources (both temporal and financial).

2. Our assessment intervention

2.1 Background

Our own assessment intervention sprang from our concern regarding the extent to which students understand assessment processes and, in particular, an interest in how we might improve student understanding of these processes, given that ever more explicit articulation does not seem to be the answer.[2] The study took place over three years[3] and focussed on transferring knowledge about assessment to students via both explicit and tacit transfer methods. The overall aim of the study was 'to improve the students' performance through enhancing their ability to assess the work of others, and, in consequence, their own work, against given marking criteria' (Rust et al. 2003, p.147).

2.2 Intervention design

The intervention was designed for a large (300+ students), first-year, undergraduate Business module. It took place during the last three weeks of the students' first term on a Business degree programme and involved them in preparation work; participation in a workshop; and submission of a self-assessment sheet together with their coursework at the end of the first term, which was three weeks after the workshop took place.

In detail, the format and timeline of the intervention was as follows:

1. One week prior to the workshop all students on the module were given two sample assignments and mark sheets including assessment criteria and grade definitions. They were asked to complete the assessment sheets by themselves, awarding a grade, marks and rationale/feedback for each of the assignments before attending the workshop.

2. Workshops lasting 90 minutes were offered to all students in groups of 40. The workshops took the following format:

    • small-group student discussion of their initial marking of the two sample assignments, to include agreeing grades and rationales for the small group;

    • feedback of small groups' agreed grades and rationales to the workshop as a whole;

    • tutor-led comparison of small groups' rationales with assessment criteria;

---

[2] See Chapter 2, section 3.2 of this book for more detail on explicit articulation and, in particular, the issues with our own criterion-referenced assessment grid.

[3] Although the paper reporting the results of the study (Rust el al. 2003) only covers data from two years.

- tutor explanation of each of the criteria;
- small group review of their agreed assessments and grade in the light of tutor explanation;
- feedback to the workshop as a whole of final grade awarded by each small group;
- provision by tutor of marked and annotated versions of sample assignments, including tutor-led discussion of assessment and marks awarded.

It is important to note that although the small groups enabled students to compare and justify their initial assessments against those of their peers, and although small groups were asked to feed back an agreed group grade/rationale, the students were specifically requested not to alter their initial grades/comments on their individual assessment sheets. These sheets were collected in for research purposes.

3. Three weeks after the workshop took place, students submitted their coursework together with a completed self-assessment sheet. The coursework gave no indication of whether or not the student had taken part in the intervention.

Again, it is important to note that the assessment sheets used for the sample assignments, the students' self-assessment, and the tutor's actual assessment of the students' work were the same and incorporated comments, a module assessment grid, and a grade and mark.

The intervention ran in three successive years with three different cohorts on exactly the same module. It was carried out in exactly the same way in all three years in order that we could make comparisons between those students who had and those who had not taken part in the workshops. We also collected data from two further modules which had similar assessment methods (a large first-year Introduction to Business Economics module which assessed students *just before* they were assessed by the Business module in which the intervention ran; and an advanced second-year Business module taken one year after the Business module in which the intervention ran).

2.3 Key indicators

Student performance

We measured student performance in the following three ways:

1. Baseline comparison of the assessment performance of workshop participants with non-participants on the Business Economics module taken before the intervention was carried out. This comparison ran in three successive years with three cohorts.

2. Treatment comparison of the assessment performance of workshop participants with non-participants on the Business module within which the intervention was carried out. This comparison also ran in three successive years with three cohorts.

3. Transfer comparison of the assessment performance of workshop participants with non-participants on a second year Business module, taken by both groups one academic year later than the Business module within which the intervention was carried out.

Initial knowledge of the assessment criteria

We gauged the students' initial knowledge of the assessment criteria and processes via their marking of the sample assignments, completed prior to workshop attendance. Their completed assessment sheets (including grade and mark awarded, rationale for this, and completed assessment grid) gave a clear indication of their application of the criteria.

Ability to self-assess

We gauged students' ability to self-assess and their understanding of level after the intervention took place via the self-assessment sheets that they submitted along with their coursework on the Business module in which the intervention was carried out. Our aim was to compare the student's self-assessed grades (overall and for each criterion) with those of the marker.[4]

[4] Unfortunately, we were only able to make use of this data in years 2 and 3 of the study. In the first year, we made an error in methodology by photocopying, for use in the study, the assessment sheets (on which the students had self-assessed and the tutor had then assessed) prior to their return to the students along with the marked assignments. This made it impossible to tell which assessments had been made by the student and which by the tutor. This error was rectified in year 2.

Effect of workshop

And finally, students completed a questionnaire to evaluate the effect of the workshop on their understanding of assessment criteria and processes, their confidence in undertaking their assessed work, and their confidence in applying the criteria to their own work.

2.4 Results

Student performance

Overall, the results of this study showed that:

1. those students who participated in the assessment workshop achieved significantly better results in their subsequent assessed coursework—and this was so for all three years of the study (demonstrated by the treatment comparison outlined above);

2. comparison of the performance of the participants and non-participants on a module run prior to the intervention (the Business Economics module) showed no significant difference in performance between the two groups (demonstrated by the baseline comparison outlined above); and

3. one year later, the participants from the first cohort of the study were still demonstrating significantly better results than those of non-participants, albeit at a slightly reduced level (demonstrated by the transfer comparison outlined above).[5]

Initial knowledge of the assessment criteria

During their initial grading of sample assignments, almost all students correctly identified that one sample was excellent and the other was poor, but a range of marks was awarded for each assignment.[6] After the first group discussion in the workshop, the agreed grades of several groups were in line with the tutor's unknown grading, and after the tutor-led explanation and small group review, several more groups adjusted their agreed grades in line with the tutor's (still) unknown

---

[5] See Rust et al. 2003, p.157 for the statistical detail relating to these results.
[6] See Rust et al. 2003, p.159 for details of marks awarded.

grading. In other words, we saw some convergence of student and tutor grading as the workshop progressed—the students' understanding of the assessment criteria appeared to grow as they moved through the workshop. Clearly, this is not, by itself, indicative of an increase in the students' assessment literacy, since we cannot say with certainty *why* the students' gradings began to converge with those of the tutor (it may have been due to increased understanding of the standards, but it may equally have been due to some other factor unrelated to their understanding). However, the fact that those students who attended the workshop continued to demonstrate better results in future years compared to non-attendees *does* indicate a growth in assessment literacy.

The students' initial individual grading attempts together with the workshop discussion indicated that they found it much easier to apply 'visible' criteria (e.g. structure, visual presentation and referencing) than 'invisible' criteria (e.g. analysis and evaluation), and they relied on the visible criteria to justify the grades that they had awarded, both individually and in small groups. After the tutor's explanation during the workshop, however, they began to apply the invisible criteria but still appeared to find it difficult to use them in justifying marks awarded, and many students noted that they found the marking task highly challenging and were concerned that they would expose their inability to assess. It seems, then, that the workshop pushed the students to start using the invisible criteria, but did not equip them with the confidence (expertise?) to make use of them effectively. We might conjecture that with more practice, gained either through further workshops, or by simply being at a later stage/year in the programme, engendering a deeper understanding of the criteria (and so a higher degree of assessment literacy), students would feel more confident— and be more able—to apply the criteria (particularly those such as 'analysis' and 'evaluation' which require a deeper appreciation of scholarly language and practice than those relating to more mechanistic issues of structure, presentation, etc.).[7] Much like Andy Northedge's (2002, 2003a) notion of academic discourse or the discourse of a discipline, assessment has its own peculiar discourse. The

---

[7] Although, as indicated under the section 'Effect of workshop', a minority of students actually felt less confident after having attended the workshop.

first step towards understanding this discourse is to learn the language of assessment, but it requires a further step to be able to meaningfully apply that language as an active member of the discourse community.

Ability to self-assess

As indicated in footnote 4, we were only able to use data relating to the students' ability to self-assess from the second year of the study. In the second and third years, the majority of students (both participants and non-participants in the workshop) gave their own assignments an overall grade, but very few additionally gave themselves a grade for each of the criteria. Initial comparison of students' overall self-awarded grade with the tutor's overall awarded grade showed little difference in ability to self-assess between participants and non-participants in the workshop (39% of participants and 45% of non-participants accurately predicted their grade; and 19% of participants and 20% of non-participants over-predicted by one grade). However, when we examined the results in more detail, we noted that when comparing overestimation or underestimation by two or three grades, there was a clear difference between participants and non-participants. Although the numbers are quite small, it is apparent that a higher percentage of non-participants overestimated the grade and a higher percentage of participants underestimated the grade. We suggest that, although on the face of it, participation in the intervention did not appear to enhance accuracy of self-assessment, there is more to this picture than meets the eye. It may well be that through the workshop and exposure to/discussion about exemplar assignments, participants became aware of the quality of really excellent work along with the relative room for improvement in their own. As a result, we conjecture, the participants underestimated the quality of their assignments (they became more critical of their own work), in contrast to the non-participants who did not have the same reference point of what constitutes excellent work.

Effect of workshop

Feedback from the questionnaires indicated that the students viewed the workshop very positively. They considered that the workshop activities and discussion had ameliorated their understanding of the marking criteria considerably. They also felt more confident about preparing for their assignments as a result (although a small minority reported feeling less confident because, having a better understanding of the level required to pass, they were now concerned about their ability to meet that level). And finally, many students asked whether the workshop could take place earlier—prior to them undertaking coursework on other modules.

2.5 Further remarks

As shown above, our assessment intervention resulted in improved student performance (indicated by comparison of the assessment performance of workshop participants with non-participants) coupled with increased confidence amongst workshop participants that they understood the marking criteria and could prepare for their assignments effectively (indicated by the results of the student questionnaire). Since all students received the sample assignments and assessment sheets regardless of whether or not they attended the workshop, and since the baseline comparison of the assessment performance of participants and non-participants failed to reveal any significant difference in performance between the two groups prior to the intervention, participation in the workshop is the only remaining factor that can account for the difference in performance between the two groups subsequent to the intervention. In other words, while it was likely that motivated rather than non-motivated students attended the workshop, the data shows that those students who attended were not, prior to the workshop, performing any better than their peers who did not attend. Attendance at the workshop therefore increased students' assessment literacy by improving their grasp of assessment criteria and standards; by developing their skills of self-assessment and peer review; and by acquainting them with basic principles of valid assessment practice, terminology used, and pertinent assessment skills and techniques. This is turn enabled them to perform better under assessed conditions. While some may argue that this is simply teaching students to 'the test', we actually believe this to be the central role of teaching (i.e. inducting students into a subject area and the methods of demonstrating knowledge and skills in that subject such that they are able to respond effectively to assessment tasks in that area), hence perfectly acceptable (indeed expected) provided the assessment is authentic and valid. Others may be concerned that our approach encourages responses to assessments that are increasingly similar when, in fact, we should be aiming to foster independent thought and alternative responses to the same question. We would argue in reply that convergence is an important aspect of student assessment literacy, since it is important that students align their mental models of 'good' standards with those of staff (their assessors). However, 'good' does not mean 'uniform'—of course there will usually be more than one possible good response to an assessment task. In order to make sure that students recognise this, it is important that we make this clear in our criteria and also that we use contrasting exemplars of good work during assessment interventions.

The intervention supported the assimilation of tacit (as well as explicit) knowledge by workshop participants via the use of exemplars (the sample assignments), practice in marking, and (particularly) the opportunity for discussion between students and with staff which aired a variety of perspectives on the meaning of assessment standards. This enabled students to gain, through socialisation, knowledge about assessment that could not be transferred via either verbal explication of the assessment criteria by staff or the written assessment criteria and grade definitions available to all students (and which were reflected on the assessment sheets circulated at the start of the intervention process). Exemplars provide a vehicle around which to form discussion of standards and criteria.

The intervention, then, is a relatively simple exercise that can be carried out within a short space of time (the current version of the assessment workshop takes only 60 minutes to run and is incorporated within the module rather than being voluntary) with a small investment of staff effort. It is effective and can be adapted to work across a range of subject disciplines. Time invested early on in this way may well pay off in the future, since students who have experienced an intervention are likely to need less support later on in their programmes. This is one concrete way in which we can work face-to-face with students, devoting some time to discussion and answering questions about the nature of assessment standards and practices, thereby enhancing both student assessment literacy and performance. As we have shown, it is possible to do this even in the face of rising student numbers and ever-diminishing staff/student contact time. And this kind of approach neatly links with the mission statements of many of today's universities—to produce independent, autonomous learners.

3. Orsmond and Merry's research

3.1 Background

Paul Orsmond and Stephen Merry have led a number of studies into methods of enhancing student understanding of assessment criteria (Orsmond, Merry and Reiling 2000, 2002; Orsmond, Merry and Callaghan 2004). Their research focuses on the role that student construction of marking criteria and (in later studies) consideration and discussion of exemplars can play in this area, as demonstrated through peer review and self-assessment activities.

The 2000 study aimed to improve student understanding of assessment criteria via discussion between students and staff, resulting in joint construction of marking criteria. Although the students were able to construct marking criteria, the study indicated that they did not gain greater understanding of the criteria as a result. More specifically, the students were asked to create scientific posters and then self- and peer assess the posters using the marking criteria that they had developed—but there was lack of agreement between the marks awarded by the students and those awarded by the assessing staff. The students and staff failed to agree on the marking standards relevant to those criteria. Orsmond et al. (2000) conjectured that this disagreement may have been due to the students' lack of familiarity with the appearance of a scientific poster, making it difficult for them to interpret staff comments about the criteria in this context. They therefore proposed the use of exemplars as a possible solution to this issue. We would further argue that straightforward construction of marking criteria by students is not sufficient to increase their understanding of assessment criteria/standards and so improve their assessment literacy, although it is a step in the right direction. As indicated by our own intervention, what is crucial for improved understanding is repeated practice in using the assessment criteria through self-assessment and peer review exercises, supported by discussion with tutors and peers. It is through this repeated use of the criteria that a student learns to think like an assessor and so comes to better understand the nature of assessment.

3.2 Using exemplars

Orsmond and Merry's 2002 study again involved construction of marking criteria by students in discussion with staff, but this time combined that activity with the use of exemplars. The study aimed (amongst other things) to evaluate the use of exemplars in developing student understanding of assessment criteria, and to provide meaningful formative feedback in relation to assessment.

The specifics of the study

Twenty-two first-year Environmental Sciences and Applied Biology students (none of whom had previously taken part in self-assessment or peer review activities at the institution) were asked to construct scientific posters under the heading of 'histology'—a topic which they had already studied. The students worked in small groups of three or four to construct their marking criteria, but they each created their own poster and marked individually.

Two weeks prior to creating their posters, the students were given verbal information relating to peer review, self-assessment and marking criteria, including being told the details of the criteria-construction and marking exercises. One week later, the student groups met with two staff members and each group constructed four criteria. They were then shown five histology posters from a previous cohort which exemplified a range of graded material—although they were not informed of the grades awarded. Students discussed the exemplars in their groups and with the staff members, then revised their marking criteria in the light of this—again having the opportunity to enter into discussion with staff. Finally, the groups wrote down the meaning of the individual criteria and handed this to staff.

The students were given 45 minutes to individually create their posters. A copy of the relevant group's marking criteria was attached to each poster. Students then self-marked their own poster using their group's criteria, and marked the poster of each person in the group using those same criteria. They recorded the grade that they awarded (1st, 2:1, 2:2,

3rd or Fail) and their rationale for awarding that grade on a 'Poster Marking Sheet' (students were familiar with this grading system via previous assignments and information supplied in the student handbook). Finally, they completed a 'Poster Feedback Questionnaire', which aimed to find out how useful the students found the exercise. The posters were marked independently by each of the staff members, without reference to the students' marking.

Results

In comparison to the 2000 study which did not use exemplars, the overall results from this study show a much higher level of agreement between marks awarded by students and those awarded by staff. Specifically, in this study:

- percentage agreement between student peer and staff marks for all poster groups ranged from 54% to 81%, and no significant deviation was found between student peer and staff mark for any of the criteria;

- percentage agreement between student self and staff marks for all poster groups ranged from 50% to 80%, and no significant deviation was found between student self and staff mark for any of the criteria;[8]

- in addition, there was a greater than 90% agreement in marking between the two independent staff markers.

The results from the questionnaire indicated that students considered the self- and peer marking exercises beneficial to their learning. They noted that discussions with staff improved their understanding and that exemplars were useful because, for instance, they showed that a poster that is visually appealing is not necessarily a 'good' poster in academic terms. Interestingly, the students considered that they would like to discuss criteria construction again in other modules, but they were less keen to repeat the process of actually constructing the criteria. Orsmond et al. (2002, p.320) conjecture that this 'may reflect the more demanding nature' of this process. We suggest that the students'

---

[8] See Orsmond et al. 2002, pp.314-5 for tables setting out percentage agreement in marking against each criterion for this study, as well as for the 2000 (and another, earlier) study.

preference echoes the point that we made at the end of section 3.1—student construction of marking criteria is not sufficient to improve student understanding of those criteria and the assessment process as a whole. It is also worth mentioning, as an aside, that most staff do not construct criteria—they simply apply them. It is the module leader who, in most cases, determines the standards and, as research by James Elander and David Hardman (2002) indicates, a staff member who has written the assessment task and associated standards is able to more comprehensively assess responses to that task across a number of aspects or attributes than a staff member who has not.

3.3 Further remarks

Given that, for both self- and peer assessment, the 2002 study demonstrates a greater agreement in percentage terms between student and staff marking for individual criteria than do previous studies in which exemplars were not used (but discussion about the criteria and student-constructed criteria were used), Orsmond et al. (2002, p.318) conclude that 'the use of exemplars in conjunction with student constructed marking criteria has enhanced the agreement between tutor and student', adding that: 'Those students marking the same as the tutor have demonstrated both an understanding of the marking criteria and the marking standard in the context of the subject matter that is the same as the tutor.' Further, Orsmond et al. argue that improving the quality of formative feedback provided to students may foster a deeper understanding of the criteria—and this process may be facilitated by using exemplars. The current study differs qualitatively from their previous ones because there is an increased focus on the use of formative feedback coupled with the adoption of exemplars as a means of providing formative feedback on student development of marking criteria. We might add that the process of using exemplars to reflect on marking criteria and adjusting those criteria in the light of that reflection provides more practice in the use (or at least manipulation) of the criteria, which leads to improved understanding.

In a later (2004) study, Orsmond et al. develop their research further, this time incorporating tutor-provided assessment criteria in addition to the various exercises (discussion of criteria, joint construction of criteria, exemplars, and peer review and self-assessment) used in 2002.

Specifically, the students were asked, in small groups, to construct marking criteria for a poster. They were then given two sets of criteria by tutors and asked to mark an exemplar poster using first one set and then the other. Subsequently, the tutors informed the students that the first set of criteria (clear logical progression; appropriate scientific content; clarity; appropriate conclusion; quality of presentation) was 'worthwhile' and the second set (colourful; simple to understand; clear title; references; conclusion) was 'ambiguous'.[9] Tutors and students then discussed the sets of criteria, with tutors further developing the concepts of criteria construction and use. Later on in the study, each student created a poster, self-marking their own poster and peer marking the posters of their group's members using the marking criteria that they had constructed in their group.

The 2004 study yielded similar results to those of the 2002 study (i.e. students were able to implement a variety of marking criteria effectively following formative discussions with both their peers and staff members), with some interesting additions:

Firstly, the students had no problems applying the 'ambiguous' criteria, but found it more difficult to apply the 'worthwhile' criteria successfully. This mirrors one of the findings of our own intervention (mentioned in section 2.4 above), namely that students found it much easier to apply the 'visible' than the 'invisible' criteria—and there is certainly some similarity between the visible/invisible and the ambiguous/worthwhile distinctions, with visible or ambiguous criteria tending to be immediately apparent to the untrained eye, and invisible or worthwhile criteria tending to be less obvious and more technical. Orsmond et al. (2004, p.284) suggest that students may find it difficult to apply the worthwhile criteria because they lack the requisite subject knowledge: 'A worthwhile criterion engages the student with the subject, and does not just focus on the construction of a poster.' As with our own analysis of the visible/invisible issue, we might further suggest that more discussion about, and practice in using, the worthwhile criteria would lead to a fuller understanding and greater

---

[9] The terms 'worthwhile' and 'ambiguous' are Orsmond et al.'s terms, not ours. In fact, we find these terms value-laden and confusing, hence would not use them ourselves.

assessment literacy, which in turn would enable the students to apply these criteria more effectively.

Secondly, while the results of the self- and peer-marking exercises using the student-constructed criteria indicated that students had an increased understanding of marking criteria and were able to apply them successfully by awarding meaningful marks (which correlated with those awarded by tutors), their written comments in support of the marks awarded did not display this level of understanding. For instance, unlike the tutor, they failed to address each criterion in turn and make comments appropriate to the criterion. Nor did their comments reflect the relevant subject knowledge. Rather, they tended to focus on the 'easier' (more visible?) criteria such as 'clarity' and 'self-explanatory' and ignore criteria such as 'appropriate scientific content' and 'meaningful conclusion' which require not only knowledge of the subject area but also a more specialised, analytical approach. Orsmond et al. (2004, p.286) argue that this does not mean that the students failed to recognise, for example, a meaningful conclusion, since the level of agreement between tutor and student marks implies that they did indeed recognise when this criterion had (or had not) been satisfied. Rather, 'recognizing something and commenting on something requires different skills.' (And, of course, this distinction applies as much to staff as it does to students.) This issue again reflects one of the findings of our own assessment intervention—that even when students started to apply the invisible criteria following tutor explanation, they still found it difficult to use them in justifying marks awarded. Again, we might argue that more practice in use and application of the criteria might go some way towards resolving this issue.

3.4 Summary

In much the same way as our own intervention, Orsmond and Merry's work indicates that it is possible to enhance student understanding of assessment criteria and standards, and so to improve student assessment literacy, via a mixture of structured activities such as construction of marking criteria, discussion of exemplars, and peer review and self-assessment. Their work is also very useful in that it illustrates the limitations of such an approach—student construction of marking criteria in itself is not sufficient to improve student understanding. What is required is reflection on and practice in using the criteria, supported by discussion between tutors and students.

4. Other relevant studies: Bloxham and West

Sue Bloxham and Amanda West conducted a pair of small studies in 2004 and 2007 aimed at (a) enhancing students' understanding of assessment criteria via seminar discussion of the criteria coupled with peer marking and self-assessment exercises; and (b) investigating whether these exercises had any long-term effect in terms of students' approaches to writing assignments. The results from the 2004 study yielded a 40% agreement between student self-predicted and tutor-awarded grades (with a further 28% of students correctly predicting their mark to within one grade), and a comparison of peer-awarded and tutor-awarded marks revealed a non-significant mean difference of just 0.4%, with tutors awarding a slightly higher mean mark than students. The students involved clearly expressed that they had gained positively from taking part in the peer marking process. Fifty per cent felt it had given them greater insight into marking and only 13% felt they had gained nothing or very little from the process.

Bloxham and West's 2007 study, which involved in-depth interviews with some of the participants in the first study, indicated that those students who had taken part in the first study subsequently paid greater attention to formal assessment information and marking criteria than students who had not taken part. The students interviewed also confirmed that they saw some value in the exercises undertaken in the first study—they had gained an understanding of how to mark and an understanding of the importance of formal assessment criteria and guidelines. Furthermore, a number of the students interviewed referred to the importance of verbal clarification for both assignment tasks and for written feedback, thereby highlighting the important role of dialogue and discussion in the development of student assessment literacy.

5. Conclusion

This chapter has looked at the kinds of pre-assessment activities that we can engage students with in order to increase their assessment literacy. The evidence indicates that if we engage students in activities that involve them in thinking about, discussing and applying the assessment criteria, they come to a fuller understanding of those criteria sooner, which enables them to perform better when undertaking assessed work. In other words, engagement with, and use of, the criteria develops an aspect of assessment literacy. And clearly, the sooner we engage our students in pre-assessment activities, the better, since becoming assessment literate is a slowly-learnt skill that develops incrementally over time—the more the student engages with and applies the criteria, the deeper his/her understanding of the criteria, and so assessment literacy, is likely to become, and the better s/he is likely to perform when undertaking assessed tasks.

We have seen that there are a number of pre-assessment activities that can be used: discussion of the assessment criteria, construction of assessment criteria by students in conjunction with staff, marking exercises, peer review, self-assessment, and use of exemplars. The studies that we have explored in this chapter typically use a number of these activities in combination to increase student understanding of assessment. Given that assessment literacy is slowly-learnt and given that different people learn in different ways, it makes sense that any deliberate intervention aimed at increasing student understanding in this area should operate on more than one front to ensure maximum (and repeated) impact. This can be achieved through a programme approach, as advocated in Chapter 3.

Our own assessment intervention is the most rigorously researched of the interventions discussed above. It is much larger than the other studies, working with a cohort of 500+ students, and the results were replicated over three years. We know that the intervention works—engaging students in pre-assessment activities aimed at increasing their understanding of the assessment criteria leads to improved assessment literacy and enables better performance under assessed conditions. (And it may well be that there is need for an intervention, not only in the first year, but also in subsequent years of a programme, when the level and complexity of subject matter and associated assessment tasks increases.) The other studies discussed are much smaller, but they still provide important additional evidence for the efficacy of pre-assessment activities in improving assessment literacy (although, unlike our intervention, they do not necessarily aim to show that better understanding of the assessment criteria leads to improved student performance).

All of the studies discussed highlight the importance of discussion and dialogue in students coming to know assessment standards. Those students surveyed felt very positive about the intervention activities and specifically mentioned how useful the opportunities for discussion were in furthering their understanding. We can take from this that explicit statement of the standards and criteria is not sufficient—students also need the opportunity to clarify those standards and criteria, to ask questions about them, and to practise applying them. It is by active engagement with the standards and criteria via exemplars within a supportive community of practice that students can develop their understanding of assessment—their assessment literacy. And it is this kind of active engagement within a community which enables them to grasp the tacit as well as the explicit dimensions of assessment practice. While this is increasingly difficult in today's world of large student numbers, limited staff/student contact time and scant resources, our intervention provides a tried-and-tested, efficient and economic means of engaging large numbers of students in activities which both enhance their assessment literacy and improve their performance. We therefore judge that the time taken to implement this intervention is far outweighed by the benefits reaped from the intervention.

Assessment Activity

1. Introduction

In this chapter we move on from the theme of the previous two chapters, planning assessment and pre-assessment activity, to the theme of actually carrying out assessment or assessment activity. Just as there are two partners in the process of assessment—staff and students—so too there are two aspects of assessment activity—that of the staff (including examiners) and that of the students. We covered the student aspect of assessment activity in some detail in Chapter 3 (Pre-assessment Activity) and, to a lesser extent, will do so in this chapter in considering possible activities during assessment. In Chapter 6 (Feedback) we will also explore the important role that peer review and self-assessment can play in the initial development of students' assessment literacy, as well as the short-term benefits that these techniques have with regard to performance in upcoming assessed tasks. When it comes to summatively assessed tasks students will be able to perform their best with a combination of disciplinary knowledge and assessment literacy and, of course, sufficient time and space to enable them to respond to the task adequately. This chapter therefore shifts perspective and mainly focuses on the staff aspect of assessment activity.

As we saw in Chapter 2, there is a need for the assessment activity cycles of staff and students to interact in order for staff to give ongoing support to student learning. However, there are two particular points where staff engagement in the cycle is critical and their assessment literacy of great importance. The first point is when staff choose the type of assessment activity or task that they will set for their students. And the second is when staff apply assessment standards by marking their students' responses to the assessment task set. We cover both these aspects of staff involvement in assessment activity during the course of this chapter.

2. Theoretical background

Elsewhere in this book (Chapter 2, section 3.4; Chapter 1, sections 2.4 and 2.5) we have put forward our own social-constructivist approach to assessment literacy. This account focuses specifically on how students come to know assessment standards, but it should not be surprising to learn that we adopt the same social-constructivist approach to staff understanding of assessment (i.e. staff assessment literacy). In particular, how staff come to understand how to make judgements about marking (Bloxham et al. 2011), as well as how they come to know local assessment standards and criteria—those standards and criteria that hold sway in the department and institution to which they belong (this will be particularly relevant in section 4 below, relating to marking).

It may be helpful, therefore, to briefly recap on our own social-constructivist approach to assessment literacy. Our approach centres on the notion of academic 'communities of practice' (Lave and Wenger 1991). Members of academic communities (staff and students) need to be encouraged to actively engage with established members in order to gain a thorough and deep understanding of assessment purposes, processes, and standards. Through active membership over time those initially on the periphery of a community should come to achieve the same level of assessment literacy as others in the community. Since much of the knowledge relating to assessment expectations and standards is tacit (i.e. cannot be explicitly articulated), neither staff nor students are able to come to a full understanding or to full literacy simply by being told about assessment. Rather, they need to be active members of a supportive community of practice in which they can ask questions of, and engage in dialogue with, more experienced practitioners and learn the local assessment mores through imitation and repeated practice.[1] Knowledge is gained through absorption, conversation and doing—and this applies to staff as much as to students.

3. Staff activity: choice of assessment task/s

In this section we examine the choice of assessment task/s by staff. By this we do not mean the surface-level choice between, for example, essays or examinations, rather we are interested in why you might choose a particular type of assessment task, or what different assessment tasks are for. In other words, we are interested in the rationale underlying choice of a particular type of assessment task. These kinds of decisions are not freestanding, however.

Firstly, they will be constrained by constructive alignment, which demands that any assessment tasks set should align with the learning outcomes and learning activities for the course or module (Biggs 1999). Thus, one of the learning outcomes for a first year, introduction to Philosophy course might be that by the end of the course students will be able to employ the basic tools of philosophical analysis. Since the majority of students will not have studied Philosophy before, it may be appropriate that any assessment early in the course be formative, aiding students in their learning and understanding, while assessment at the end of the course be summative, testing whether students actually have understood how to employ the basic tools of philosophical analysis, and thereby whether they have satisfied the learning outcome for the course.

Secondly, decisions about assessment task have to be made within the context of the overall programme (see Chapter 3 for a detailed discussion of programme-level assessment). In other words they need to take into account the requirements of the programme, which will include things like whether assessment is to be integrated or not, what the balance between summative and formative assessment should be,

---

[1] And, in some cases, question and challenge the local assessment mores, thereby possibly introducing new ways of doing things.

the areas to which limited resources should be directed, etc. One such example that is particularly relevant in the context of this book is group work, which will need to be designed within the overall programme and balanced effectively with, for example, individual work. (Note, though, that as explained in Chapter 3, programme design is informed by the overall institutional context, hence the institutional context will also influence the design of individual assessment tasks within a programme.)

The mode of learning that a course aims to deliver also forms part of the overall programme context and will therefore inform decisions about assessment task. Is the mode of learning face-to-face, distance or blended? The way in which we deliver feedback to students, for example, will be constrained by the mode of learning employed on the course. If the mode of learning is face-to-face, then we can relatively easily provide face-to-face as well as written feedback. But if the mode of learning is by distance, it becomes more difficult to deliver feedback. We might perhaps consider providing written feedback in the first instance, combined with the opportunity for a telephone call with a tutor to provide a forum for discussing that feedback further.

Thirdly, there are a number of further, interrelated considerations that have to be taken into account when choosing assessment tasks:

Consideration 1

Consideration one relates to engagement. Is the point of a particular assessment task to engage the students in the work that they are doing, to encourage them to approach the work in one particular way rather than another? Will the task help to motivate the students? Will it challenge them? If the point is to provide some kind of formative feedback mid-course, then the assessment task will need to be engaging and interesting enough that the students actually partake in the assessment. If it is formative, they also need to learn something from doing the assessment. This means that the task should be versatile enough that it challenges the most able students, whilst motivating (rather than disengaging) those who are less able, or who have a weaker grasp on what has been taught so far. A final summative assessment will have less to do with engagement/motivation (the fact that the task is summative should be motivation enough in most cases) and more to do with fairly and adequately assessing what has been taught, as well as being rich enough to reflect different levels of student performance, knowledge and ability.

Consideration 2

Consideration two relates to feedback loops. The giving of feedback[2] has become so important in the assessment process that David Nicol has stated that the first thing staff need to think about when designing a course is at which points feedback will occur, i.e. at which points students will receive feedback and be given the opportunity to act on that feedback. Clearly, feedback and its timing will impact heavily on the choice and nature of assessment tasks. Thus, for example, one might choose an assessment task involving initial draft/giving of formative feedback/redraft/submission for summative assessment, thereby building a feedback loop into the assessment activity for that course.

Consideration 3

Consideration three revolves around knowing your students. This means being cognisant of what your students know already when they join the course. But it also means being aware of how homogenous your students are in terms of knowledge, or being aware of how their knowledge is distributed. This was neatly illustrated by Lewis Elton (1997) in terms of the humps of a camel (or, more technically, a bell curve). One common scenario is that most students' knowledge falls in the middle of the spectrum with a small number of students knowing very little and a small number of students knowing a lot. This results in a one-humped camel.

Another possible scenario is that a significant proportion of your students knows a lot, another significant proportion knows a little, with a small proportion falling in the middle with a mid-level of knowledge. This results in a two-humped camel.

More generally, consideration three involves the notions of adaptability to the needs of different students and of equal opportunities. Thus it will be important to be aware, for example, of cultural diversity, since

---

[2] See Chapter 6 for a detailed discussion of feedback.

students from different cultures or home countries may well come to your course with different knowledge levels and learning styles, not to mention different English language abilities. It is important that all students, regardless of background, are provided with equal opportunities to learn.

Consideration 4

The fourth consideration involves manageability. A decision needs to be made regarding what kind of assessment is suitable or appropriate given factors such as the size of the class, the length of the course, and the speed with which feedback needs to be given. For example, in a very large first-year module with several hundred students it may simply not be manageable from the staff/marker perspective to employ an assessment task which involves each student producing a written assignment requiring detailed, individualised marking and feedback. In this situation, it may be necessary instead to employ assessment tasks that involve, for example, use of generic feedback; or student self-assessment; or peer assessment. Assessment tasks that are framed in this way in this situation are manageable.

Consideration 5

The fifth consideration takes into account independent learning, or learning to learn. This relates to the long-term effects of the assessment, and is about skills rather than the application of disciplinary knowledge. These skills comprise generic life skills such as research skills, or group work skills, or presentation skills. We may want the assessment in a course to support independent learning; to help equip the students with these independent learning skills. In this case, both the course and the assessment need to provide the students with the requisite tools to continue learning by themselves. For example, some kind of self-assessment may be appropriate, whereby the students learn to critically assess their own work against that of others and of themselves so that they become good judges of their own performance and understand how they can improve that performance. And this kind of self-assessment is, of course, more than simply a method for assessing what has been learnt; it is also a form of learning in its own right—learning how to self-assess for life.

4. Staff activity: marking

In this section, we explore the second area of staff assessment activity—marking. We begin by looking at the shift within higher education in recent years from norm-referenced marking to criterion-referenced marking and we focus on the issues associated with each approach. We then introduce our own community-of-practice-based approach to marking, explaining how this encourages objectivity of assessment standards and criteria, whilst answering some of the issues associated with current approaches to marking.

4.2 Criterion-referenced versus norm-referenced assessment

As we have seen elsewhere in this book, there has, over recent years, been a move within higher education to make assessment standards more transparent and consistent (both within and across institutions)—a move which has been prompted by widespread concern about equality and fairness. The focus has been on making standards explicit via written statements covering learning outcomes, level descriptors and disciplinary benchmarks.

This has had a corresponding effect on the practice of marking and there has been a move from 'norm-referenced' assessment or marking whereby the performance of a student is judged against that of his/her fellow students to 'criterion-referenced' assessment or marking whereby a student's performance is judged against a set of explicit, written criteria and standards. The arguments in favour of criterion-referenced assessment are that it is fair (each student is judged against the same set of standards), consistent (all staff use the same set of criteria and standards to judge their students' work), avoids arbitrary staff decisions (staff can be seen to be accountable for the marks that they award), is transparent and justifiable (it is possible to point to the standards and criteria and say this is why that student was awarded that mark), and makes it easier for students to grasp the standards that they are expected to attain. Under criterion-referenced assessment, the decisions that assessors make about students' performance are underpinned by something external (explicitly stated criteria and standards) to the assessor. Therein lies its apparent objectivity.

On the face of it, this sounds convincing. Marking is probably one of the most important tasks that staff perform in relation to students. After all, the marks that a student receives can determine the classification of their award, or at least give an indication of the quality of their learning in the subject, and ultimately impact upon their future career opportunities. Of course staff want to get it right—they want to be fair and consistent and award grades that correctly reflect student achievement across the board. But is criterion-referenced assessment the ultimate panacea? Research suggests not.

Researchers have, in fact, identified a number of issues with criterion-referenced assessment. One such issue questions the fundamental tenet of criterion-referenced assessment—that assessment standards and criteria, objectives and outcomes can be written clearly and explicitly such that there is no room for doubt about their meaning and, importantly, that markers can be in no doubt about what grades they should award, having read the standards and criteria. However, empirical research indicates that there is, in fact, considerable variety in the grades that different markers award to the same piece of student work (Ecclestone 2001; Yorke 2008). Furthermore, there is a good deal of variation in the way that different markers interpret terms such as 'analysis' or 'evaluation' (the kinds of terms that are commonly used in statements of assessment criteria)—and this is particularly the case in relation to interdisciplinary dissertations and projects (Saunders and David 1998; Webster et al. 2000).

The criterion-referenced approach to marking does not, then, seem to lead to more consistent or reliable marking. This issue, of course, links back to the point that we made above (and which we discussed in detail in Chapter 2) that knowledge about assessment and assessment terms is largely tacit—it cannot be clearly and explicitly articulated in the absence of some kind of prior knowledge or understanding about the assessment process and the particular context in which it occurs. In the case of assessors, this kind of understanding might be gained through, for example, some kind of discussion or agreement, as illustrated through exemplars, about the meaning of terms such as 'analysis' and 'evaluation' prior to commencement of marking. Without this kind of background understanding or agreed reference point, exact meaning cannot be gleaned simply from reading written descriptions.

Another problem with criterion-referenced assessment is that of comparing standards across disciplines and, indeed, institutions. What might an A grade level of 'critical thinking' look like in history, or mathematics, or chemistry? What might these different, disciplinary, manifestations of critical thinking share in common that we could define them all as a grade A—and how could we write this down clearly and unambiguously? Empirical research indicates that currently this kind of consistency simply does not exist. Thus Yorke, Bridges and Wolfe 2000 found that the percentage of first class degrees awarded across disciplines ranged from 21.1% in mathematics to 3.7% in law, while another study indicated that marks awarded for arts subjects such as English and history created a very different mark distribution from those awarded for more quantitative disciplines such as mathematics (Bridges and Bourdillon 1999).

It has been argued that these kinds of issues are addressed by internal and external moderation, which ensures fairness of marking within disciplines and across the sector. Moderation is certainly valuable in that it encourages open discussion about assessment criteria and marking decisions, and provides staff with the opportunity to view their peers' marking. However, researchers suggest that it has its limitations. These include (for internal moderation) power relations between staff influencing decisions about moderation (Orr 2007) and (when the mark awarded by the first marker is unknown to the moderator) a tendency to act cautiously and award average marks (Hornby 2003). With regard to external moderation, moderators are at a disadvantage because they do not know the context in which the students have done their learning (Price et al. 2010). Other problems relate to the difficulty of the external moderator's role given the increase in complex, modularised degree programmes across the UK; differences between types of institution; lack of experience on the part of moderators leading to an inability to compare standards across institutions; and the lack of time available for non-bureaucratic quality assurance procedures that engender discussions of standards and a community of practice. Yet another issue is to what extent external moderators can be considered to represent the view of their community, as opposed to their own individual views.

Criterion-referenced assessment, then, seems to have many problems. Although it strives for objectivity and reliability, we have learned that it is not always objective or reliable. There is a lack of consistency between markers and across institutions, there are problems with understanding the meaning of apparently explicit statements of assessment criteria, and marking/moderation decisions may well be influenced by factors quite independent of the quality of students' work and how that quality relates to the published criteria. Furthermore, and rather interestingly, a number of researchers have highlighted the fact that markers find it almost impossible to mark without comparing one piece of student work with another (Wolf 1997; Bloxham et al. 2011). This is echoed in work by Laming (2004) who argues that human judgement fundamentally relies on comparative processes rather than on objective, standardised measures. This recourse to norm referencing may well be due to the difficulty of interpreting and applying a set of written standards in a vacuum, as noted above. Markers need to learn how to apply those standards, and this knowledge comes from other staff members and feedback from moderators and external examiners, but largely from the range of work that different students produce where the standards are most clearly manifested.

What, then, of norm-referenced assessment? Norm-referenced assessment (the general term for assessing a student's performance relative to that of a group rather than against a set of criteria) and grading on the curve (a specific, more formal type of norm-referenced assessment) are both designed to compare students' performance with that of their peers.[3] Students' performance is ranked in order to determine final grades. The more formal grading on the curve approach does this by dispersing the students' marks along a bell curve. The marker then uses the resultant 'normal distribution' to award grades to the students. The proportion of grades at each level is predetermined, ensuring that the proportion of grades awarded at each level remains constant year on year.

[3] Many sources conflate the terms 'norm-referenced assessment' and 'grading on the curve', although they are, in fact, subtly different, as indicated above.

The most damning argument against grading on the curve revolves around the notion of the 'normal distribution'. With an enormous data set it may be reasonable to expect that students' marks would produce such a bell curve. However, it makes no sense to therefore assume that every group of students will perform in this same way, regardless of size or other context.[4] It has also been pointed out that such a distribution is more likely to be a random rather than a 'normal' result. Thus Grant Wiggins (1993, p.154) points out that 'the norm curve...is the distribution most appropriate to chance and random activity' as opposed to what we might reasonably expect from the purposeful activity of students studying a course together—that the majority succeed in doing well. Much the same point was made twenty-five years earlier by Benjamin Bloom (1968): 'The normal curve is a distribution most appropriate to chance and random activity. Education is a purposeful activity and we seek to have students learn what we would teach. Therefore, if we are effective, the distribution of grades will be anything but a normal curve. In fact, a normal curve is evidence of our failure to teach.'

Other criticisms of norm-referenced assessment include that it reveals nothing about overall standards and fails to reflect very high or very low levels of achievement, since all achievement is measured relative to one's peers. For example, it may be that a whole cohort performs particularly poorly. In this case, those who performed best would still receive an A grade, even though their assessed work shows weaknesses —and even though their marks/level of knowledge may well be less than those of students who were awarded an A grade in previous years (assuming overall cohort performance was better in previous years). Conversely, in a cohort displaying very high levels of performance, only those students who perform best (i.e. attain the highest marks) will receive an A grade, even though the performance/marks of some of those students receiving lower grades may be just as good as that of students awarded A grades in previous years (assuming cohort performance was poorer in previous years).

---

[4] And, in fact, compare this with Lewis Elton's one-humped versus two-humped camel discussed under 'Consideration 2' above.

And finally, the random nature of norm-referenced assessment can make it very difficult for students to make sense of their own performance. We can imagine a situation in which coursework is not graded on the curve, but where the final, end-of-course assessment is graded on the curve. In this case, it could, for example, be that a student receives very high marks throughout their course and therefore reasonably assumes that they will be awarded an A grade at the end. Yet, if their peers perform very well (and better in a number of cases), that student may well end up with a B grade when graded on the curve, simply because the requisite proportion of A grades has already been awarded to those with the highest marks.

It is also worth mentioning that norm-referenced assessment provides no incentive for staff to improve their overall student performance, since this performance will never be judged in an absolute sense, but always in terms of the normal distribution, or in terms of the students' performance relative to one another. Neither does it provide any incentive for students to work together or collaborate with one another, since under norm-referenced assessment they will always be in competition with one another.

4.3 A community-of-practice-based approach to marking

There are clearly a number of problems with both criterion- and norm-referenced assessment. How, then, should we ensure that marking is as objective and reliable as it can be? How should we ensure that staff hold a shared understanding of the criteria that should be applied when making marking decisions? After all, staff do not, in general, appear to be in a quandary about the quality and consistency of their own marking. A study by Sue Bloxham and Pete Boyd (2011, p.1) revealed that 'tutors believe there are established and shared academic standards in existence in their discipline and they endeavour to maintain them.' Where, then, do those standards reside and how can markers become fully conversant with them?

Our answer is that those standards reside in local communities of academic and assessment practice. It is through participation in a community of practice that staff come to understand the assessment standards and practices of their institution and their discipline. New staff will acquaint themselves with the standards in this way; established staff will refresh their understanding and make sure that it incorporates new and revised standards in this way. It is through participation in a community of practice that staff absorb the tacit knowledge that enables them to grasp the meaning of the institution's and the discipline's written statements of criteria and standards. And it is through participation in a community of practice that staff learn to understand and interpret those written standards in the same way, to apply them consistently, and so to ensure fair marking decisions for their students. Of course, this process of absorption of standards is not always easy, not only due to limitations on staff time and logistical issues, but also where the community fails to recognise or include some staff (such as associates or PhD students), yet it is a vital process and, as Handley, den Outer and Price (2012, p.12) explain, participation provides '...a vantage point onto the practices, implicit values, rituals and structure of the local practice.' It is therefore incumbent on higher education institutions to recognise the importance of community (developed through mutual engagement: dialogue, team working, etc.) and promote, defend and resource time for it.

Academic standards are not, we believe, something external or independent in the positivist sense of those terms—something 'out there', waiting to be discovered and codified. How could they be when the standards are something created and agreed by academic communities? But this does not imply that the standards are purely subjective, nor that they will (or should) simply vary from marker to marker. Rather, they are negotiated within an academic community of practice and they are influenced by markers, but they exist independently of individual markers. The objectivity of the standards lies in the fact that they form part of the 'collective consciousness' of a community of practice, thus are not dependent upon the subjective decisions of individual markers.

So, how, in reality, do staff members come to know the assessment standards of their institution/department/discipline via participation in one or more[5] academic communities of practice? Clearly, there are a

---

[5] Some staff may, of course, belong to more than one community of practice depending on disciplinary and programme affiliations.

number of ways in which the community can facilitate this learning—
through formal induction or training; through more informal activities
such as participating in marking meetings, attending exam boards,
discussing students' work with colleagues; and through very informal
activities such as conversations with colleagues and students about
assessment tasks and standards over a cup of coffee or 'at the water
cooler'. An exploratory study by two of the current authors (Handley,
den Outer and Price, forthcoming) provides insight into which
methods are considered to be useful. This study, which examined how
nine new members of staff (including salaried staff, hourly-paid
contract staff, and bursaried and non-bursaried PhD students) to a UK
Business School came to understand the local assessment practice,
indicated that, across the board, these new staff found one-off, formal
induction and training events to be of limited value. Rather, what they
found to be much more useful were informal interactions, which they
actively sought out such as sitting in on others' classes; in-depth
discussions comparing marking of and feedback for the same
assignments; marking meetings to discuss students' work; pre-teaching
meetings to discuss the aims of the assessment tasks and the module
in general; and, more generally, an 'open door' policy that enabled
them to seek out and speak to other staff members. The new staff
valued these informal interactions as opportunities that enabled them
to participate in the community and gain a wider picture of assessment
in the Business School, as well as giving them the chance to evaluate
their own judgements about assessment in this new environment.

Furthermore, the Handley et al. (2012) study emphasised the interesting
relationship between the proximity of staff's physical work base (i.e.
where their desk was, which often related to their employment
contract) to the hub of the community, and the development of staff
understanding of assessment standards. Being physically co-located
with other staff obviously makes it easier to converse, collaborate with
and ask questions of one's colleagues but also, more subtly, physical
co-location encourages a sense of belonging to the academic
community of practice which, in turn, gives individuals the confidence
to interact more readily with their colleagues. Thus, the salaried staff
and bursaried PhD students in the Handley at al. study, who had office

space in the centre of their departments, generally felt confident about asking questions, making suggestions, and attending events such as exam boards. In contrast, the hourly paid contract staff and non-bursaried PhD student, who were allocated desks in communal space away from the centre of the department, felt much more reticent about interacting with and asking questions of their colleagues. Handley et al. describe the relations that these staff did experience as largely 'transactional'.

Some concrete examples of attempts to facilitate staff understanding of assessment standards—and to establish the standards themselves—via participation in an academic community of practice also exist.

The Hospitality, Leisure, Sport and Tourism Network (HLST), a Higher Education Academy Subject Centre, was inspired by our own work on assessment standards and community[6] to run three workshops aimed at bringing staff from different institutions within the same disciplinary area together to discuss specific issues on assessment standards. The first workshop focused on the characteristics of final year undergraduate HLST subject assignments assessed at the threshold of first class work, and involved approximately twenty academics across HLST subjects and from a range of UK universities coming together, first to assess work in small groups and then to discuss and agree standards as well as the assessment process itself. Those who attended the workshop considered such discussion about assessment standards and information sharing within disciplinary areas and across institutions to be highly valuable. The second workshop built on the first, this time concentrating on threshold standards (i.e. marks of just over 40%). Tutors from ten UK institutions took part in an exercise to determine specific characteristics of student work that would merit a threshold pass mark. Finally, the third workshop focused on the differences between dissertations awarded a 2.1 grade and those awarded a 2.2 grade, using the final year undergraduate dissertation as a focus for the discussion. Again ten HLST academics met, first to re-assess individually dissertations originally awarded a 2.1 or 2.2 and then to agree as a group criteria that differentiated the two grades. They

---

[6] See Chapter 7 of this book for further details on our work on community.

also discussed these differences with a group of students who had recently submitted dissertations. The workshop participants agreed that, if widely-understood standards relating to the assessment of student dissertations were to be implemented, sharing of current practice was essential. They therefore proposed that marking schemes, guidance provided to students, and different approaches to supervision should be shared via the HSLT website.[7]

In Australia, as part of the Achievement Matters project (2010), and inspired by our work as well as that of the HLST, Phil Hancock and Mark Freeman are leading the Accountancy discipline in trying to establish national standards by means of 'a national model of expert peer review'. This pilot project will initially involve Accountancy departments from ten Australian universities, but the project outcomes will subsequently be offered to all other Australian Accountancy degree providers. As an integral part of this process, the project seeks to establish a 'Reference Group' of national and international experts in assessment and academic standards for Accountancy which will work together to 'develop and implement a national model of expert peer review for benchmarking learning outcomes against nationally-agreed thresholds for the accounting discipline'. Outcomes of the project will include 'external peer-reviewed evidence of accounting academic standards in all types of higher education providers, benchmarked against the accounting threshold learning outcomes'; 'a model process for obtaining and using blind external peer review evidence'; and 'professional learning and capacity building'. It is hoped that these outcomes will enhance quality assurance procedures; provide an inclusive and reliable model that can be adopted by other disciplines; and provide professional development for academics (Hancock and Freeman, personal communication).

---

[7] See http://www.heacademy.ac.uk/hlst/resources/a-zdirectory/positionpapers for details of all three workshops and the position papers resulting from them.

4.4 Summary

To summarise, while we support the notion of criterion-referenced assessment, we believe that its successful implementation depends on community rather than the spurious belief that criteria can be made explicit. Academic standards, we believe, reside in academic communities of practice. These standards are agreed by members of the community of practice (operating at local, national and international level) and it is this communal agreement and collective ownership that renders them objective rather than subjective.

Since these standards are objective, it is possible for staff members to come to know and understand them in such a way that the standards can be applied consistently by different markers. However, due to the tacit nature of assessment standards, such understanding or staff assessment literacy can only be gained by immersion within an academic community of practice which owns the assessment standards. Immersion encourages dialogue between members of the community and participants in assessment activity, which enables newcomers to 'acclimatise' to the community and thus, over time, to come to know its assessment practices, standards and criteria fully and be able to apply them consistently. We believe that, in order for this to happen effectively, participation in the community and dialogue between its members needs to be encouraged. And, of course, the assessment literacy of the community as a whole must be nurtured. Participation can be encouraged by providing opportunities for newcomers to become involved in assessment at all levels—from developing criteria, learning outcomes, module materials, etc.; to attending and contributing to meetings about marking, student progress and exam boards; to ensuring that seasoned staff are available and willing to talk to others about assessment. These kinds of opportunities will not only foster a culture of dialogue, interaction and constructive questioning but will also foster a sense of belonging for new community members, which will further encourage their participation thus allowing them to develop more quickly a deeper understanding of the local assessment practices and standards.

5. Student activity: self- and peer assessment

The same benefits in developing students' assessment literacy that can be obtained through activities pre-assessment (as discussed in Chapter 4) can also be achieved through self- and peer assessment activities whilst undertaking the assessment task, focussing on the student's judgement of quality while in the act of production (of the assessment product).

5.1 Building a feedback loop into the assessment process through peer review

Following the success of the marking intervention (described in the previous chapter) we decided to apply the same thinking to helping the students engage with, and learn from, feedback (Price et al. 2007) through the introduction of a peer-review workshop. This voluntary workshop was offered a week before the submission date for the assignment so students had to have completed their assignment a week early. A peer-review checklist had been given to the students one week before with the suggestion that they might also use it to guide self-review of their own work before attending the workshop. At the workshop, students worked in triads. They had 40 minutes in which to read one other member of the triad's work, guided by the peer-review checklist, and to record their comments on a peer-review form. They then had 15 minutes each (i.e. 3x 15 minutes) to give and discuss that feedback, with the third member of the triad encouraged to listen and contribute too. The incentive to complete their work one week early and to attend the workshop was that those attending and attaching the peer-review sheet to their finally submitted work would be awarded 3 extra marks (out of 100). This was felt to be the smallest mark that would provide an incentive while not having an undue effect on the final mark. It was also intended that there was the additional incentive that students would be able to revise, and thus improve, their work in the light of the feedback received.

Both the students and the course tutors (assessors) evaluated the experience positively—and both groups overwhelmingly believed the workshop had been beneficial. In particular students saw the highest benefit from seeing examples of others' work rather than feedback on their own work. We would hypothesize that this provided information with which they could review their own work. However it has to be admitted that, in terms of hard evidence, the results of this intervention were somewhat disappointing, in that we failed to demonstrate any measurable improvement in the work of the students who attended the workshop compared with those who did not. One possible, and we believe plausible, explanation—especially as these were first year students—is that the attendees adopted a strategic and instrumental approach and, reassured by the peer-review process, concluded that their work was sufficiently good enough to pass (and with grades essentially unimportant) and so were prepared to settle for 'good enough' this time.

5.2 Taylor

Suzanne Mary Taylor (2011) describes a peer-review exercise which occurs mid-assessment, in that it was conducted mid-semester, which did demonstrably result in improved student performance.

In setting the scene, Taylor explains that the (largely summative) assessment regime for a Financial Accounting module (with approximately 1,400 students a year) at Queensland University of Technology failed to motivate students since it did not provide opportunities for formative assessment or feedback, nor did it allow students to participate as partners in the assessment process. Consequently, it was decided to replace the mid-semester exam in semester one with a peer-assessed, weekly assessment task. This provided the students with valuable learning opportunities, enabling them to act as primary assessors. Taylor explains that, specifically, students benefitted from the speed and quality of the formative feedback that they received, the opportunity to see what constituted the preferred solution to the assessment task, the opportunity to see the different approaches adopted by their peers to the assessment task, and being asked to judge whether and how the work of their peers met the marking criteria. She also reports that student performance increased significantly after the mid-semester exam was replaced by the peer-assessed task, with overall failure rates dropping by 15%, tutorial attendance and rates of engagement rising to approximately 100%, and

100% of students rating the peer-assessment exercise positively in confidential surveys carried out at the end of the module.

5.3 Further examples

There are other examples in the literature of peer review and self-assessment activities that have been used to improve student understanding of assessment criteria and self regulation, but few of these provide concrete evidence for a further link between such activities and improved student performance. For a useful list of other peer review and self-assessment studies, see Falchikov 2005, Chapter 5. Falchikov (2005) also provides an extended discussion of ways in which to involve students in assessment, including exploring issues such as how well students are able to judge their own work, and how reliable/valid student peer assessments are. For an example of how training in self-assessment practices has been shown to improve the quality of work amongst high school students, see McDonald and Boud (2003).

6. Conclusion

As well as considering student activities during the assessment task which may help to develop student assessment literacy, we have in this chapter mainly looked at staff assessment activity. In particular, we have examined (1) the kinds of considerations that staff face when setting assessment tasks and (2) the two extant approaches to marking student work—the criterion-referenced and the norm-referenced approach. We have seen that there are deep inadequacies associated with each of these approaches. We have therefore introduced our own alternative community-of-practice-based approach to marking which, in our view, provides a more objective and reliable model for marking and assessment practice.

Post-Assessment Activity: Feedback

1. Introduction

Having discussed pre-assessment activity and assessment activity in Chapters 4 and 5, we are now in a position to discuss post-assessment activity—carrying the learning forward via feedback. It should be noted that it is often most appropriate and effective for feedback to occur *during* assessment rather than post assessment. However, for sake of simplicity, this chapter considers feedback as a post-assessment activity.

This chapter begins by considering the role that feedback plays in developing assessment literacy, and by examining the nature of feedback and its purpose. Having established that feedback is key to student learning, we explore how and why so many students have negative experiences of feedback. We then turn to how this can be changed for the better, arguing that it is necessary to focus on increasing students' levels of engagement with feedback, which will thereby increase its effectiveness. We give some practical examples of how feedback could be improved in order to heighten student engagement and feedback efficacy. Finally, we set out our own analytical stages of engagement model, which depicts the various stages of engagement within the feedback process including points of and reasons for disengagement. We conclude by correlating the stages of this model with our suggestions for improvements to the feedback process.

2. The role of feedback in assessment literacy

The literature tells us that formative feedback is, arguably, the most significant aspect of the assessment process by dint of its potential to affect future student learning and achievement, and to develop deeper student understanding of assessment standards (Hattie 1987; Higgins et al. 2002; Gibbs and Simpson 2002).

Throughout the course of our lives (both everyday as well as within an educational context) feedback provides us with a strong indicator of how we ought to proceed. Feedback comes from, amongst others, family members, friends, peers, teachers, colleagues and authority figures. We expect and accept feedback from these quarters and use it to reflect on our past actions, as well as to shape and inform out future actions, speech, thoughts and opinions. At the most basic level, a child learns right and wrong (it is wrong to hit another child who has snatched a toy) via feedback from others (a parent's admonishment, the other child's cry of outrage/pain).[1]

It is no surprise, then, that feedback plays an equally pivotal role within formal education. Whatever we consider the role of feedback to be—reinforcement, correction, benchmarking, or guidance for future appropriate action (and, in reality, it is likely to be a little of all of these things)—feedback (effective feedback, at least) should enable us to reflect on our past performance and adjust our future performance in the light of the feedback, whether that is at the level of writing the next assignment or at the level of further developing cognitive skills and understandings.

In Chapter 1, we discussed the term 'assessment literacy'. We asserted that, amongst other things, assessment literacy involves

---

[1] Of course, mere receipt of feedback does not guarantee that the recipient learns from the feedback. The further step of reflection on the feedback provided is required for learning, as well as to distinguish learning from mere conditioning (where someone changes their behaviour without reflection). Thus, following the model of Kolb's (1984) experiential learning cycle, in order for learning to occur, an individual needs not only to have a concrete experience, but also to observe and reflect on the effects of that experience, thereby forming an understanding of the general principle governing the particular experience (abstract concept formation), which can be actively tested and so in turn leads to new experiences.

(1) a conceptual understanding of assessment (an understanding of the basic principles of valid assessment and feedback practice), (2) familiarity with technical approaches to assessment (familiarity with assessment and feedback skills and techniques), and (3) understanding of the nature, meaning and level of assessment criteria and standards, which entails the ability to select/apply appropriate approaches and techniques to assessed tasks. Clearly, then, effective feedback should play a key role in developing assessment literacy. Receiving and reflecting on feedback should aid a student in developing their conceptual understanding of assessment—they will begin to understand the practice or process of receiving and using feedback as an integral part of assessment and learning. Reflecting on, and making use of, effective feedback (i.e. actively engaging with the feedback) should familiarise the student with technical approaches to assessment, as well as strengthen their grasp on the subject discipline. They will begin to understand the nature and purpose of feedback, including how it can be used to improve future performance and enhance learning. And finally, a student should, through reflection on effective feedback, come to have a deep understanding of the assessment criteria and standards. This in turn should enable them to choose between different skills and techniques in order to approach an assessment task appropriately and successfully.

Feedback, then, is essential for the learning process and for becoming assessment literate. And, as we shall see in the remainder of this chapter, feedback must be engaged with by the student in order to be effective.

3. What is feedback?

The term 'feedback', much the same as the term 'assessment literacy' (see Chapter 1, section 2.1), is commonly used but does not have sufficient clarity of meaning, either in the pedagogic literature or in practice.

Up until the late 1960s, feedback's primary role was seen as reinforcement. This view was informed by the dominant behaviourist perspective whereby knowing was equated with observable connections between stimuli and responses, and learning with the strengthening or weakening of those connections via reinforcement and non-reinforcement (Greeno et al. 1996). Behaviourists such as Skinner (1968) thus viewed feedback as a strong external stimulus providing positive or negative reinforcement to behaviour.

In the early 1970s, behaviourism was superseded by a cognitivist view of learning which held that there exists a fixed body of knowledge and that learning involves accurately reflecting how things 'really' are in the world. Cognitivists considered that feedback provides information (leading to a more accurate body of knowledge) and identifies and corrects misconceptions (about the way things really are). Under this interpretation, feedback is a one-way communication or transmission with the 'expert' tutor providing information to the 'novice' student in order to help them learn (Askew and Lodge 2000).

Both the behaviourist and cognitivist perspectives suggest that feedback is an unambiguous response and can provide incontrovertible corrective action (much like a thermostat acting as a feedback loop in a heating system)—but this is rarely the case with educational feedback, especially within higher education. As we saw in Chapter 1, the kind of learning demanded in higher education is complex and high level and, correspondingly, its assessment tasks require performances that are multi-dimensional (Yorke 2003). Feedback must, therefore, reflect the complexity and multi-dimensionality of the performance. Furthermore, feedback is provided within an assessment process that rests on both partially-explicated criteria and professional judgement (O'Donovan et al. 2008; see also Chapter 2 of this book). As a result, assessment standards are unclear, which leads to the possibility of ambiguity regarding feedback—and there is limited mileage for ambiguous feedback to 'correct' complex work.

Sadler (1989) moves beyond a purely corrective notion of feedback to suggest that while feedback identifies errors and misunderstandings, it also has a very important forensic role. By this he means that feedback diagnoses problems with student work; or provides information about the gap between actual and expected performance in a manner which aids the student in closing the gap. Under this interpretation, then, feedback also has a benchmarking role. Whether feedback really can aid the student in closing the performance gap will depend, however, on the nature of the gap. Where the gap relates to some concrete element, such as curriculum content, feedback should be able to clearly specify the missing content. Yet where the gap relates to a more nebulous element—the need to further develop some academic or cognitive skill, for example—feedback may be unable easily to suggest how to immediately close the gap, since such skills are learnt gradually, through the acquisition of tacit as well as explicit knowledge and do not lend themselves to explicit articulation (see Chapter 2, section 3 of this book).

Hattie and Timperley (2007, p.82) suggest that, in making sense of the various interpretations of feedback above, it is useful to 'consider a continuum of instruction and feedback'. Feedback provided at different points on the continuum is likely to serve different purposes. At one end, there is a clear difference between giving instruction and giving feedback, whereas when feedback takes on a correctional (or instructive) role, 'the feedback and instruction become intertwined' and the process of giving feedback itself becomes a new kind of instruction—a process which involves supplying information (instruction) about how to fill Sadler's performance gap.

Recent research moves to another point along the continuum, arguing that feedback in higher education must focus on developing new ways of knowing (Lea and Street 1998) and there seems to be emerging consensus that feedback should explicitly address future as well as current work (Gibbs and Simpson 2004; Torrance 1993). In other words, feedback should be formative in nature—it should '"feed backwards" to help students analyse and critique their completed assignment against the assessment criteria; as well as "feed forwards" to help students develop the capabilities appropriate for possible future assignments' (Handley et al. 2008, p.11). With the focus on future as well as current work, feedback acquires a longitudinal role and its temporal dimension becomes significant. Feedback is usually interpreted, not in isolation, but in the context of an individual's knowledge and previous experiences. It may also be re-interpreted in the light of future experiences. Its longitudinal nature means that effective feedback can support improved performance in a student's next assignment(s), but also (and perhaps more importantly) guide and support the development of slowly-learnt literacies (Knight and York 2004) and threshold concepts (Meyer and Land 2006). The notion of feedback as longitudinal and formative in nature therefore puts paid to the limitations of a purely forensic notion of feedback, as sketched out in the paragraph above.

4. Problems with feedback

We have established in section 2 above that feedback plays a significant part in developing assessment literacy. And clearly staff spend much time and effort generating assessment feedback, whatever they view the ultimate purpose of that feedback to be.

What, then, of the student attitude towards assessment feedback? Research has shown that students are keen to receive feedback (Hyland 2000; O'Donovan et al. 2001), both that which helps them to achieve better results in future assignments and that which helps them develop generic, deep skills (Higgins et al. 2002; Hodgson and Birmingham 2004)—they are keen to receive feedback that is formative in nature. However, many are dissatisfied with the feedback that they receive. In the UK, for example, recent results from the National Student Survey indicate that students, almost universally, rate assessment and feedback lower than other aspects of higher education courses. Furthermore, the literature shows that students do not necessarily engage with the feedback that they receive: 'it is not inevitable that students will read and pay attention to feedback even when that feedback is lovingly crafted and provided promptly' (Gibbs and Simpson 2004, p.20). Why is this?

Various studies have highlighted a number of problems with feedback in higher education. In her 2001 study, Maclellan found that 30% of students surveyed said that the feedback supplied never helped them, and most said it only helped sometimes. Other studies have shown that students find feedback too vague, subject to interpretation, or too subjective (Higgins 2000; Ridsdale 2000; Holmes and Smith 2003). Hounsell (1987) found that students do not read the feedback supplied, while Lea and Street (1998) revealed that even when feedback is read, it is often not understood. This may be due to its inherent jargon and complexity, or to a lack of student understanding of the assessment criteria. The timing of feedback may be inappropriate—it is often provided at a time when students no longer consider it useful (Juwah et al. 2004). In other cases, it appears that where the emphasis of feedback is on the mark or grade awarded, the student may construe this as relating to their personal ability or worth, rather than to the worth of the specific piece of work, which can result in poor marks damaging the student's 'self-efficacy' (Wotjas 1998). And finally, Fritz et al. (2000) have shown that feedback that is passively received in the absence of any tutor discussion may have no effect at all—when students were asked to repeat the same assessment task at a later time, they completed it largely as they had done before, including replicating their earlier mistakes.

The net result of these various problems is that many students find it difficult to engage with the feedback given, and this is because the feedback does not meet their expectations. Some students do not even pass the first hurdle of picking their written feedback up! While feedback has considerable potential to enhance student learning, that potential is not being harnessed, and many students appear to give up on feedback, despite the fact that they believe it to be an integral part of the educational service that they are receiving (Higgins et al. 2002).

5. Changing feedback for the better

As we noted in section 4 above, staff spend much time generating feedback and students are enthusiastic about receiving feedback, yet at the point of engagement, the process breaks down. What can we do to improve this situation?

5.1 Conceptual background

Before answering this question, it is helpful to sketch out our conceptual approach to (student engagement with) feedback. In Chapter 2 (section 3.4), we set out our 'cultivated community of practice' model of how students come to know assessment standards. This rested on a number of interlinked assumptions: the importance of communities of practice in learning, which reflects the socio-cultural nature of learning and knowledge; the importance of engaging students as active participants in the assessment process; the necessity of students participating as partners within a community of practice in order to develop a full understanding of the assessment standards within their discipline.

We adopt a similar, social-constructivist approach to feedback (see, for instance, Rust et al. 2005). The assumptions implicit in this approach are as follows:

- staff and students are active participants in an interactive feedback process. Students actively seek to construct meanings based on their own experience and beliefs, formulate their own learning goals, and engage in actions to achieve those goals in a continuous reflexive process (Nicol and Macfarlane-Dick 2006, 2004);

- feedback is not simply linear communication, but involves complex 'issues of emotion, identity, power, authority, subjectivity and discourse' (Higgins et al. 2002, p.272); and

- assessment and feedback are culturally and contextually situated. They take place, for instance, within institutions constituted in—as well as being sites of—discourse and power (Lea and Street 1998).[2]

So, we believe that feedback should be a dialogue between staff and students—it is not simply a case of the assessor issuing written comments on a piece of work and, conversely, engagement with feedback is not the responsibility of the student alone. This dialogue does not take place in isolation, but within an environment or community which will impact on the content and delivery of the feedback. In the words of David Nicol (verbal communication), a dialogue does not mean a duologue—dialogue involves much more than a two-way conversation.[3] Furthermore, the nature of the feedback given will be influenced by the knowledge, previous experience, expectations and personality of the staff member giving the feedback and, of course, how the student interprets and acts on that feedback will depend, in turn, on his/her knowledge, previous experience,

[2] These assumptions are taken from Handley et al. 2008, p.14.
[3] A dialogue can also, of course, take place between two students.

expectations and personality. Feedback is therefore, in our view, a thoroughly complex, social process.

5.2 Feedback as process versus product

Earlier in this chapter we discussed the meaning of the term 'feedback' and noted that feedback's role was seen as reinforcement (by behaviourists) and correction (by cognitivists). Such approaches typically construe feedback as a product. By this, we mean that feedback is seen as something generated by a tutor in response to a piece of student work. It is bounded and applies only to that piece of work—once the feedback has been generated, the job is done.

In contrast, social-constructivist approaches such as ours view feedback as a process (see the student and staff cycles of the assessment process set out in Chapter 2). In many senses, the generation of the feedback is simply part of an ongoing process of engagement, reflection and action (more detail on this process is given in section 6 below, where we set out our stages of engagement model of feedback). The process is initiated by the student receiving and then engaging with feedback, which may (or may not) prompt them to reflect (Where could I improve? How could I improve? What skills do I need to develop further? How can I apply what I have learnt in my next assignment?), and then to act (I will further develop my skills of critical analysis by attending the study skills session run by my tutor next week. I intend to structure my next assignment in the following way to increase the clarity of my argument.), which in turn influences further reflection and action in relation to future feedback. As a result of engaging with feedback, the student performs more effectively and becomes more assessment literate. And so the process continues.

5.3 Improving feedback: focussing on engagement

We know that students seek feedback. We know that feedback is generated from a number of sources—staff, self and peers. And we believe that feedback is a socially constructed process. How can we improve the effectiveness of feedback? The key, we believe, is to kick start the process so that more students are engaged. It is only once students are fully engaged that they will (can even) reflect on and use feedback, and it is only once they start doing this that the efficacy of feedback will increase.

As Valerie Shute (2008, p.175) points out, effective feedback relies on three factors: motive, opportunity and means. In order for feedback to be effective or engaging, students must need the feedback, they must receive it in time to have an opportunity to use of it, and they must be willing and enabled to make use of it. If students do not have an opportunity to apply feedback, or do not understand it, or judge it to be irrelevant, they will not engage with it.

Harnessing engagement is essentially about sparking someone's interest in an issue, which involves that person understanding the issue, what it means for them, and why it is worth their while engaging with it. In the words of Handley et al. (2008, p.24): 'Students engage with what is potentially useful to them. . .there needs to be an expectation that the lessons drawn from engaging with feedback can be applied elsewhere.'

We suggest below that there are a number of ways in which feedback practices can be improved, and these address some of the problems raised with feedback earlier in the chapter. The result should be more useful and more practical feedback which actively engages and incentivises the learner, leading to a greater capacity for learning and assessment literacy.

The ways in which we suggest feedback practices might be improved fall into two areas as follows:

5.3.1 Preparing students for feedback

Preparation for feedback is best done as soon as possible in a student's course, i.e. during their first year, so that they can derive maximum benefit from the preparation and from the feedback itself early on.

Align expectations

As we saw earlier, there exist different conceptual positions about the nature and purpose of feedback and, inevitably, tutors have different views about the nature of feedback, as do students. A three-year FDTL5 study across three Business Schools in UK universities: 'Engaging Students with Assessment Feedback' (see final project report: Handley et al. 2008) indicated that the majority of staff surveyed considered feedback to have a developmental purpose, with several others recognising the benchmarking role of feedback, with the emphasis on feedback justifying the grade. Frequently, however, formative and summative assessment were conflated, which led to confusion among both staff and students about the purpose of feedback. Ultimately, primary emphasis fell on the summative, and the formative aspects of assessment were negated. Staff therefore espoused the view that feedback has a longitudinal, developmental role, but reported practice highlighted its benchmarking and forensic role.

The study showed that few students considered their grade to be purely synonymous with the feedback (although they were confused when the feedback appeared at odds with the grade). Some considered feedback as 'giving you a push in the right direction' rather than being able to make everything perfectly clear. Very often students expressed the wish that feedback should be something to help them do better in the next assignment, and some wished for more specific feedback.

There appears, then, to be a mismatch between student and staff views about the purpose of feedback, with students wishing for specific feedback that they can apply in the next assignment, and staff believing that feedback should have a long-term role in developing broader assessment literacy, while actually using feedback in its benchmarking sense to justify the grade awarded and to highlight performance gaps. This mismatch creates confusion and frustration on both sides.

Our first suggestion for improving feedback, then, is to align expectations between staff and students and between teams of markers. It is vital to specify clearly the purpose of feedback so that markers share the same understanding of why they are giving feedback and students share that same understanding in relation to the receipt of feedback and the ways in which it can help them. From a student perspective, aligning expectations should begin to harness engagement since it enables them to understand what feedback is and why it is of benefit to them. It is worth noting that the purpose of feedback may vary from assignment to assignment, so it is not enough to align expectations just the once— it has to be done each and every time (Freeman and Lewis 1998).

Identify all feedback available; model and encourage application of feedback

There is a perception that feedback means written feedback, and that this is the only form of feedback available. And, indeed, formal feedback does generally come in written form, even if it is the summation of orally delivered comments—perhaps as remarks written on an assignment, or as a completed tick box sheet, or both. However, there are other types of feedback available, some of which are already being used in higher education (albeit to a limited extent).

Handley et al. (2008) identified a number of different types of feedback that can actively engage students. Firstly, student engagement with feedback is enhanced in cases where they can apply formative feedback given on draft assignments prior to final submission. Secondly, students are more likely to engage with the assessment criteria when they embark on phased assignments involving other formative elements such as pre-submission peer reviews or phased on-line discussions. Thirdly, students found exemplars of previous assignments helpful in order to understand the standard of their work by comparing it to that produced by others. Indeed, they wanted to engage in discussion about criteria and standards in relation to these exemplars, rather than simply downloading them. In all these examples, the students saw the benefit of engaging with these more varied feedback methods in terms of improving their performance and developing deeper learning.

It is also important to emphasise the very significant role that oral feedback can play. Oral feedback may come from either the tutor or from peers. For example, the tutor may give generic, oral feedback in class, or students may take part in a peer discussion about written feedback on one of their assignments. Oral feedback is particularly important, since it moves feedback from being a product to a process in which students can be actively engaged. Feedback is no longer something 'done' to a particular piece of work but is a process or practice in which students can voice their opinions, ask questions of their tutor and peers, compare their work to that of others and so on. Students begin to move into the academic and disciplinary community of practice and to explore their own understanding of assessment.

However, we need to be aware that students may not consider oral feedback to be feedback, largely due to the informal manner in which it tends to be given (they may, for instance, take a brief corridor conversation about an assignment to be nothing more than a friendly chat). It is therefore important to stress to students the role of oral feedback and the various forms that it may take.

Require and develop self-assessment

It is important that students should be able and willing to assess the quality of their own work. In order to be actively engaged with feedback, they need to be able to take responsibility for the work that they produce, as well as having the ability to critically assess it in the light of feedback provided. The three types of feedback identified in the previous section all encourage the development of self-assessment, since the student is required to review his/her work in the light of tutor or peer feedback and to consider how exemplars might relate to his/her own work.[4] Another means of developing self-assessment (and one which may help with the self-efficacy issue identified in section 4 above) is to provide only comments but no mark or grade on a piece of submitted work. The students are then asked to identify the grade from reading the comments, and are only given the actual grade awarded once they have done this. This encourages them to practise and develop their assessment literacy.

5.3.2 Ensuring feedback is fit for purpose

Not only do students need to be prepared for feedback, in the sense of understanding its purpose, being aware of the types of feedback available and how to use them, and being self critical, but the feedback that they are given must be clear, relevant and useful.

Clear communication/usability

At the most basic level, feedback should be clearly communicated to the student. The structure, purpose and meaning of feedback comments (both written and oral) should be as clear as possible, although there will, of course, be greater opportunity for students to

---

[4] See Chapter 4 of this book for a discussion of self-assessment across a variety of contexts.

seek further clarification, ask questions, etc. in the context of oral feedback. Feedback comments must be usable—they should include clear explanation about the performance gaps exhibited as well as focus on skills development for future work (Walker 2009). This, of course, assumes that both the actual and target performance (assessment criteria) can be explicitly articulated, and it is not always clear that this is the case (see Gibbs and Dunbar-Goddet 2007 as well as previous chapters in this book). The Handley feedback study showed that students only find feedback presented in the form of written grids/rubrics useful in cases where they already understand what the assessment criteria mean—where they are already assessment literate. These points are indicative of the limitations of written feedback used in isolation, and they also highlight the necessity of being assessment literate in order to make sense of feedback. Feedback given in the absence of assessment literacy leads to confusion.

The tone of the feedback should be appropriate. It should be pitched at a level and in language that matches the stage of learning of the students. The students' perception of the delivery and tone of feedback is also significant. Where the tutor intends feedback to be developmental and for the student to enter into dialogue, for example, the tone used should encourage such an approach—it should encourage participation in the community of practice. Use of the imperative is likely to discourage this approach by reinforcing the novice–expert divide.

A student is only likely to engage with feedback provided they can read/hear the feedback clearly, can interpret the language used, and do not feel distanced from the community or belittled by the tone of delivery.

Timeliness

One of the issues identified in section 4 above was that the timing of the feedback should be appropriate. Students need to see that there is an opportunity to apply the feedback provided, and soon—generally in the next assignment. In other words they need to have the opportunity to develop their assessment literacy with the feedback provided.

We can ensure timeliness of feedback via a variety of methods. One possibility is to give initial 'quick and dirty' generic feedback to the class as a whole by describing overall strengths and weaknesses, highlighting what was done well and what needs to be improved. Students can then evaluate their own work in the light of the generic feedback, thereby developing their assessment literacy, and the tutor can give individual feedback that builds on the earlier generic feedback at a later stage. Another possibility (as described in section 5.3.1 above) is to provide initial feedback on a draft, with the students redrafting in the light of that feedback, and so again developing their assessment literacy.

Oral feedback/dialogue

We have already touched on the limitations of written feedback in the section 'Clear communication/usability' above. In addition, research has shown that if a student fails to understand the feedback given, simply providing more and more written feedback in an attempt to clarify does not help—indeed it may have the opposite effect of overwhelming and therefore discouraging the student (Brown and Glover 2006; Walker 2009). Oral feedback can be more useful in that it allows for effective expansion on the written—students may further explore the feedback given by engaging in discussion with the tutor and one another, by asking questions, by seeking clarification of terminology, concepts, etc.[5] Oral feedback is also likely to be helpful when a tutor seeks to define or explain concepts that do not easily lend themselves to explicit articulation, since it enables extended elaboration on a subject, which written feedback does not. These kinds of concepts tend to be slowly-learnt academic or cognitive skills, such as criticality or analysis or logical argument. We cannot define these skills in a few simple words, not least because they encompass a whole host of tacit understandings and experiences that are grasped over time through active engagement with the appropriate standards within a community of practice (see Chapter 2, sections 3.3 and 3.4).

Increasing the opportunity for dialogue about feedback will render students active participants in the feedback process, which should thereby increase their engagement as well as developing their overall assessment literacy (and even in time-poor environments it may be

---

[5] Oral feedback can, of course, be given by the tutor in class, but research indicates that audio feedback can also be helpful (see http://sites.google.com/site/soundsgooduk/).

more effective to spend five minutes giving face-to-face feedback to a student than to provide five minutes' worth of written comment). We can introduce opportunities for dialogue in the process via, for example, in-class discussion of exemplars, peer-review discussions that are supported by tutors, and learning sets (where a small group of students meets regularly to discuss issues and to learn together).[6]

Community

In Chapter 2 (section 3.4) and in section 5.1 above we discussed the important role that communities play in learning—providing environments in which novice members can engage with more seasoned members and thereby acquire an understanding of the practices and language of the community through observation, discussion and imitation. Community also has an important role to play in relation to feedback. For example, if students are actively engaged in a community of practice, we might expect them to feel more confident about approaching staff, entering into dialogue with them, asking questions about feedback provided, and discussing how they might apply that feedback in future work. We know that students are more inclined to accept and act on feedback from staff they know and trust, and a community of practice can nurture such relationships amongst its members. And the feedback that students receive is seen as part of the community's interactions integrated into the whole ongoing learning process rather than being a final somewhat isolated element of the assessment process. In general, we would expect a community of practice to support student learning about, and understanding of, assessment and feedback practices, along with the associated language and terminology. The existence of a community of practice is therefore likely to enhance the effectiveness of feedback practices.[7]

Linking assessment strategies

Handley et al. (2008) indicated that in highly-modularised degree programmes students see limited opportunities to apply feedback. This is because modularisation tends to limit the extent to which assessment can be closely linked across modules, and students may see no

---

[6] See Chapter 4 for more detail on these methods.
[7] This is something that we touch on again in Chapter 7.

opportunity to apply feedback from one module to the next. In addition, the study showed that some students consider that each tutor has unique assessment preferences, with marking between tutors considered as inconsistent. So, students may view feedback received on one module as inapplicable to another, especially if it is taught by a different tutor. In this scenario, students are unlikely to engage with the feedback at the end of a module, because they can see no benefit from engaging (no opportunity to apply the feedback in future work).

We therefore suggest that it is important to review and if necessary to develop programme assessment strategy to improve the linkage of assessment between modules/units. In this way, students will see the benefit of engaging with the feedback received, since they will be able to apply it to future work in other areas of the curriculum. Furthermore, increased linkage of assessment strategies should result in more coherent and consistent programmes of study which should encourage and support slowly-learnt skills and deep learning over time, thereby supporting the longitudinal role of feedback and the development of assessment literacy.

5.3.3 Summary

We began section 5.3 by asking how the effectiveness of feedback could be improved. Our argument has been that, in order to increase effectiveness, it is first necessary to increase students' engagement with the feedback provided. Since people engage with things that they can see the benefit of engaging with, and since students tend to engage with what they consider useful in terms of being applicable to the next assignment, it is necessary to improve the usefulness of the feedback (in student eyes). We have suggested that feedback practices can be improved on two fronts: first by more adequately preparing students for feedback and second by ensuring that the feedback provided is fit for purpose. Our suggestions should result in a common understanding of the purpose of feedback among staff and students; an understanding of the various kinds of feedback available, and particularly the value of oral feedback and shared dialogue; a heightened ability amongst students to self-assess; and feedback that is clear, useful, timely and can be applied across programmes and modules. Such feedback should be useful to the student, in the sense of being applicable to future work as well as aiding development of deep learning over time, and (due to better preparation) the student should realise that it is useful. The result should therefore be increased student engagement with feedback leading, in turn, to more effective feedback and an enhancement of assessment literacy.

6. Feedback and the analytical stages of engagement model

We have discussed in practical detail how to improve feedback practice, heighten student engagement and thereby improve the efficacy of feedback. It is also helpful to examine the process of student engagement from an analytical standpoint. In Price, Handley and Millar (2011) we provide a detailed analysis of student engagement data via a simple stages of engagement model. This model depicts the various stages of engagement, shows how one stage leads to the next, and sets out why a student may engage or disengage at each stage.

6.1 The model

The stages of engagement model builds on the work of Chinn and Brewer (1993) which reframes engagement as a process in which students have choices of action. This conception is helpful since it enables us to ask at which stage we can influence a student's choices and what the best way of doing this might be. The model sketches the stages in the process of engagement leading to a considered student response (choice of action).

Figure 6.1 (opposite) is a simplified version of the model which depicts the various stages of engagement (collection, immediate attention, cognitive response, and immediate or latent action), as well as the possible outcomes at the end of the process (immediate specific action, developmental changes, and rejection).

Each stage in the model is a necessary precursor to the next, but each does not necessarily play an equal role in terms of engagement. The extent to which a student passes through the process provides some indication of the extent of his/her engagement. In an ideal world, of

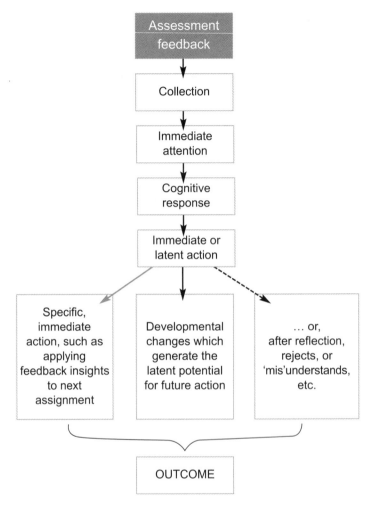

Figure 6.1: Student experiences and responses to assessment feedback [8]

course, the student would follow the entire process and fully engage with the feedback, but we know in reality that a student can disengage at any stage. Full engagement will depend on achieving the right balance of multiple factors (some of which are discussed in the sections on ways of improving feedback above), but this is hard to find, and it may be easy to discourage engagement or trigger disengagement if the

---

[8] Both figures 6.1 and 6.2 (overleaf) first appeared in Price, M., Handley, K. and Millar, J. (2011) 'Feedback—focussing attention on engagement'. *Studies in Higher Education 36(8)*, 879-96.

balance or combination of factors is wrong. The student who fully engages will, each time s/he passes through the process, gain more understanding of the role of feedback in assessment, thereby becoming more assessment literate.

Finally, it is important to note that, for simplicity, figure 6.1 does not depict the socio-cultural context which we believe to be critical in influencing the nature of the student experience (see section 5.1).

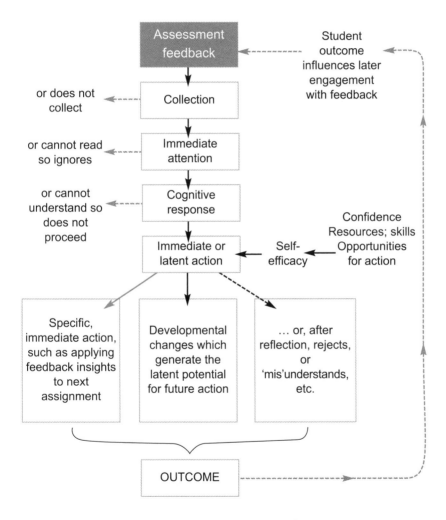

Figure 6.2: The temporal dimension of student engagement with assessment feedback

Figure 6.2 (opposite) is a fuller depiction of the stages of engagement model and indicates how a student may disengage at each stage, as well as showing that the outcome at the end of the process affects the student's engagement with feedback at a later stage.

The findings discussed in Price, Handley and Millar (2011) indicate that many students become increasingly disengaged with feedback as they progress through their university careers as a result of repeated, unsatisfactory feedback experiences. Disengagement, then, does not appear to be an immediate response, but builds up over time. Each stage of the engagement process can trigger further engagement or disengagement. In fact, engagement in the early, visible stages (collection, immediate action) is not necessarily indicative of engagement at later stages, since early on, students may be struggling to integrate feedback received with their learning (perhaps due to some of the problems listed in section 4 above). When students feel that feedback may not be useful for their learning, their disengagement becomes apparent at earlier stages in the process (they may fail to pick feedback up, for example, or may throw it in the bin on receipt).

The points of disengagement and the reasons for disengagement are as follows:

Stage 1: Collection

This stage is the most visible indicator of the student's intention to engage. The data indicated, unsurprisingly, that where a student considers feedback to be useful, they will collect it. Where there is diversity of assignment tasks in a programme, or where the tasks are set by different tutors, students consider the feedback less useful (they cannot apply it directly to the next assignment), and they are therefore less motivated to collect it (see section on 'Linking assessment strategies' above). It was common that previous unsatisfactory feedback experiences created an unwillingness to collect.

Stage 2: Attention

Once a student has collected some feedback, s/he may choose to attend to it or not. Those students surveyed were clear that illegible or mechanistic (tick box) feedback did not attract attention and was not retained. However, when students judge feedback to be usable, the level of attention that they pay to it will depend on many factors including the nature of their relationship with the tutor and the extent to which they feel embedded within a community of practice (see section 5.1 above); how easily they can understand the feedback; and immediacy of opportunity to apply the feedback to future work.

Immediate attention is likely to be affected by the student's emotional response to the mark awarded or the tone of the feedback. In the same way as anyone else, when a student receives a more critical appraisal of his/her work than expected, this can often bring a reluctance to engage with the detail. We hope that in the way that staff finally brace themselves to look carefully at reviewers' comments on a submitted journal article, students will return to their feedback and engage with it in order to improve subsequent work.

Stage 3: Cognitive engagement

Once the student has attended to the feedback provided, the next and most critical point of engagement is the extent to which they consider this in relation to their learning. Student expectations and beliefs about the nature and purpose of feedback are most significant at this point— and how assessment literate a student is will affect those expectations and beliefs. Those students surveyed appeared to understand the temporal dimension of feedback, realising that it could be relevant in the long term (and not just applicable to the next piece of work).

However, despite the fact that many students had engaged with feedback at earlier stages in the process, their expectation was of specific directive feedback, indicating that they saw themselves as recipients of a product rather than as active partners in a learning process. They were less willing to engage at the cognitive stage because of the need to make autonomous decisions about future work following developmental feedback that had been provided. Whether students were able/willing to engage at the cognitive stage largely depended on the extent to which they understood the nature of the subject and the nature of the feedback (how assessment literate they were) and on their self-efficacy (their judgement of their ability to attain certain goals). As a consequence, students often reported that they needed reassurance that their understanding of the feedback was correct; even those who had understood were limited in their ability to proceed without further help, which in turn limited the usefulness of the feedback. And this was a good indication of lack of assessment literacy amongst these students.

Those students surveyed clearly indicated that cognitive engagement is best supported through dialogue with staff. However, this dialogue is often impeded, with staff availability and attitude being the most common barriers. Students identified staff approachability as a vital factor, but many students did not have the confidence to raise questions with staff or to engage in dialogue with them (the ability to engage in discussion about assessment presupposes some degree of assessment literacy). Those who did reported that their questions were sometimes not answered, leading them to feel rebuffed.

The cognitive stage of the engagement process is critical, but also perhaps the most difficult to encourage and support. Both students and staff need to have a clear understanding of feedback, including an understanding of feedback as process rather than product, as well as opportunities for dialogue and an environment which supports long-term intellectual development and assessment literacy. It is, however, possible to structure activities that demand reflection into the process, which makes it more likely that students will cognitively engage (Quinton and Smallbone 2010).

Stage 4: Taking action

Even where a student has been fully engaged at each of the earlier stages, it does not necessarily mean that they will take action. This may be so for a number of reasons. Feedback may be rejected because of failure to understand or because of self-efficacy issues which prevent action. Other students may understand the performance gap highlighted by feedback, but do not currently have the capacity to be able to fill that gap. They will need further help in order to apply that feedback—for example, if feedback says they need to 'develop analytical skills further', tutor support may be required in order to increase both self efficacy and skills. There may be no immediate opportunity to apply the feedback given. Or it may be that a student has already fully developed their skills of critical analysis over time, has evaluated the feedback provided, and made a reasoned decision to reject it. Whatever action a student takes (or fails to take) will inform the next feedback cycle.

6.2 Linking the model with improvements to feedback

The stages of engagement model is helpful since it enables us to understand the various stages of engagement, how one stage leads to the next, and how engagement results in (in)action. It also enables us to understand at which points and why students may disengage and how engagement may be better encouraged and supported.

Last of all, it is possible to directly relate the stages of the model to the ways in which we believe feedback can be improved (discussed in section 5 above). In this way one can easily see how the suggested improvements can impact on each stage in the process (note that some improvements may impact on more than one stage). This relationship is most simply depicted in a table, as follows:

Feedback Stage	Improvements
Collection	Good preparation early on: Align expectations re nature/purpose of feedback Identify all feedback available (including oral) Model/encourage application of feedback Develop self-assessment
Attention	Clear communication Usability Timeliness
Cognitive engagement	Align expectations re nature/purpose of feedback Develop self-assessment Clear communication Usability Importance of oral feedback Importance of dialogue Importance of community Design in activities that compel engagement
Action	All of the above!

Table 6.1: Feedback: stages of engagement and suggested improvements

7. Conclusion

This chapter has provided a detailed and wide-ranging discussion of assessment feedback and student engagement with it. We have:

- explored feedback's role in developing assessment literacy;
- examined various conceptions of the nature of feedback;
- set out various problems that have been identified with feedback as it currently stands;
- made a number of suggestions for improvements to the feedback process which centre on better preparing students to receive feedback and ensuring that feedback provided is fit for purpose; and
- introduced our own model of the stages of student engagement with feedback, including directly relating each stage in the model with our suggestions for improvements to feedback.

It is apparent that feedback plays a pivotal role in student learning and that, in order to improve student learning and assessed performance, it is important to get the feedback process right. An assessment literate student is one who understands the value of feedback. We believe that improvements can be made to the process which will increase student engagement with feedback and thereby improve its efficacy. The result should be better performance (in the shorter term) coupled with deep learning and understanding over time.

Community

1. Introduction

In the previous three chapters we have discussed practical ways of enhancing students' assessment literacy at different stages in the assessment (and teaching and learning) process—pre-assessment, during assessment, and post-assessment. In this chapter we move on to discuss a concept that underlies all stages of assessment and the learning experience as a whole—that of community. In Chapter 2 we introduced the notion of a community of practice in which students actively participate alongside staff in order to become conversant with the assessment standards, processes and practices of their discipline. Integration into such a community of practice is, we believe, fundamental in supporting students' development of assessment literacy.

This chapter therefore explores the notion of community in more detail by attempting to define it, examining why it is important to focus on community (including citing some of the research evidence in support of community), and looking at ways in which community can be cultivated (drawn from our own efforts and experience). Since there is a dearth of literature on the subject of how, in practical terms, community can be cultivated, we take a case study-based approach to this particular question throughout the chapter.

2. What is community?

The concept of community is both complex and contested. There also exist different, overlapping communities. For example, a student might be a member of the community of their cohort, of their discipline, of mature students, of the rock climbing society, and so on. In simple terms, however, communities can be either looser or denser (Wellman and Wortley 1990) and coalesce around either territorial or relational dimensions, although clearly these two aspects are interrelated (Gusfield 1975). Lave and Wenger (1991, p.98) describe community as a 'set of relations among persons, activity, and world'. Drawing on situated learning theory they conceptualise a community of practice as newcomers moving towards full membership and participation in the practice of a community through mutual engagement and interaction, a sense of shared enterprise, and a common repertoire of resources (including discourse). There are, however, inherent tensions in applying this organisational concept to higher education and, in particular, in mapping out the role of students within academic communities. What practice are students coming to know—that of their subject discipline (accountancy, history, sport science) or the practice of learning itself within their discipline? These are often very difficult to disaggregate and, even more challenging, how can students be encouraged to engage with a community that they may well see as alien and unwelcoming?

As evidenced in Chapter 2 (indeed throughout this book), our interest in community springs from our endeavour to develop students' understanding of learning and assessment practices—their assessment literacy. It also springs from our commitment to a social-constructivist viewpoint, which highlights the fundamental role that engagement with a community of practice plays in teaching and learning. In the sections below we therefore set out some pointers for encouraging students to engage in the academic community of practice.

3. Why should we focus on cultivating academic community?

In this section we briefly explain (a) why we consider the development of a community of assessment practice to be so important and (b) why we are interested in developing students' sense of community in more general terms.

As we have already seen in previous chapters, an indispensable condition for students doing well in assessments is for them to hold the same conceptions of quality as their tutors. In other words they need to understand terms such as 'excellent' and 'good' in the same way as their tutors—and this is precisely the outcome that our assessment intervention (described in detail in Chapter 4) aims to secure. However, the nature of 'excellence' is not transparent and tutors struggle to define clearly and unambiguously what constitutes an excellent piece of work. One of the reasons for this concerns different interpretations of particular qualities or criteria. As we saw in Chapter 1, different individuals will, when asked to define a specific term such as 'criticality' or 'analysis', come up with different definitions (Webster et al. 2000)—and the more diverse the group (in terms of discipline, nationality, educational experience, etc.), the more diverse the definitions are likely to be (O'Donovan et al. 2004). As we also saw, further complications arise in relation to explicit articulation of standards. How can we describe the difference between, for example, 'good' analysis at undergraduate and postgraduate level in a way that does not invoke relative terms ('deeper', 'more complex') or relative concepts (the degree of student autonomy involved)?

As discussed in detail in Chapters 2 and 4, terms such as 'excellent' and 'good' involve tacit understandings of assessment standards and criteria, hence their meanings cannot be explicitly articulated. Such tacit understandings are shared at a local level through social processes involving practice, observation and imitation (Nonaka 1991). This sharing, we argue, is likely to be achieved most effectively in close academic communities of practice where the density of both formal and informal interactions amongst staff and students is enhanced (O'Donovan et al. 2008). It is through repeated interactions within a supportive community of practice that novices can best observe, imitate, practise and ultimately pass on the community's understanding and practice of assessment. And this is why we consider a community of assessment practice to be so important—it provides and supports the kinds of experiences and interactions which are crucial in developing assessment literacy amongst the student body.

A number of international research studies also underline the role that community plays in enhancing student learning in a wider sense. Foremost amongst these is Astin's rigorous, large-scale, 1993 study which aimed to determine what 'matters in college education' and involved approximately 25,000 students, 20,000 academic staff and over 300 institutions in the US. The research framework consisted of a multiple regression analysis of 146 student characteristics on entry to university; 192 environmental variables including institutional, course, policy, faculty and peer characteristics and experiences; and 82 outcome measures in terms of student characteristics after exposure to the university environment. Astin found that student interactions with faculty and particularly their peers was the most potent of the environmental variables in terms of a positive effect on students' overall growth and development (1993). Interestingly, this research indicated that institutional characteristics matter only to the extent that they structure and encourage peer and faculty relationships and interactions. This confirms the outcomes of earlier work in which Astin suggested that students who not only devote considerable energy to their studies, but also participate in community—spending much time on campus, participating actively in student organisations and activities, as well as interacting often with faculty are the most likely to demonstrate strong educational gain (Astin 1984).

More recent research from Australia and the UK provides further evidence in support of the role of community. Studies using Rovai's questionnaire on students' sense of community evidence the importance of community in decreasing attrition rates and student burnout in many different contexts (Rovai 2002; Rovai and Jordan 2004). Gibbs et al.'s (2009) research into departments rated excellent in both research and teaching highlights the importance of a focus on student involvement in ensuring joint success in these areas. As set out in Chapter 6, our own research (Price, Handley and O'Donovan 2010) emphasises the importance of dialogue and the perception of a relational dimension to feedback in securing student engagement. All of these studies, then, indicate that community matters in a broad sense—positively affecting student satisfaction, student retention, student engagement, and even the overall success of university departments. Clearly, community is crucial, not only for developing students' assessment literacy, but also for fostering students' wider social involvement and participation at university, which encourages academic engagement and in turn supports academic success.

4. How can community be cultivated?

In the previous section we argued that communities are important vehicles for fostering student engagement which in turn will support the development of assessment literacy and learning but, as we noted in Chapter 2, it is not immediately clear how to initiate a community of practice and there are few practical road maps suggesting how we might cultivate stronger academic communities for both students and staff.

However, Wenger et al. (2002) argue that a community's evolution can be 'shepherded' via provision of structures, activities and opportunities that promote and support participation, as well as give physical space for enhanced interaction. Similarly, Rust and Smith (2011, p.120) argue that 'acceptance of the principle of a true academic community of practice has clear implications for the management and structure of institutions', including, for example, organising staff and students into manageable subject groupings and providing bespoke physical accommodation (including generous informal spaces) for all the activities (teaching, learning, research, administration) associated with these groupings. Astin (1993) also urges higher education institutions to rethink their approach to education and support pedagogic and structural reforms that foster student involvement and interaction with peers and faculty, since peer and faculty interaction has been shown to be crucial in securing student satisfaction and engagement with learning.

We have taken these pointers on board and have endeavoured, as a case study, to cultivate a community of assessment practice within our own institution which focuses on two main areas of activity:

1. Provision of affinity space in which social learning can take place and the opportunities for informal and impromptu interactions are enhanced.

2. Provision of intentional opportunities for dialogue, interaction and collaboration both within and outside the formal classroom.

4.1 Context

We have supported and contributed to assessment research and initiatives throughout the UK and internationally, but the context for our development of community has been the undergraduate programmes of the Business School at Oxford Brookes University. The Business School has very large undergraduate class sizes and is located on a satellite campus, a bus ride away from the central hub of the university. These two factors combined mean that students spend a relatively small amount of their time on the satellite campus, coming for lectures and seminars but then leaving again quite quickly, preferring to socialise elsewhere, closer to the heart of the university (Kiddle 2009). These issues promote an impersonal environment in which students can feel isolated from their tutors and their academic community, hence the Business School offers a real challenge and an ideal landscape for experiments in cultivating a sense of community and belonging as an affiliate to enabling a community of assessment practice.

4.2 Getting started

Our first task was to determine any pre-existing sense of community within the Business School and then to decide on the level at which such a sense of community should be cultivated. As a baseline we were interested in finding out whether Business students felt any sense of community or belonging to either their institution, school or disciplinary programme. Our early surveys (O'Donovan and Price 2007)—replicated over two years and eliciting 488 responses from undergraduates at the end of their first year—indicated that only 40% of students felt a strong sense of belonging, and this was to the institution, not to their school or programme. They attributed their affinity to interactions and relationships forged in their halls of residence and/or via sports activities and student societies. The other 60% of students felt no, or very little, sense of belonging, attributing this to lack of personal relationships and dialogue with staff, large class sizes, living off campus and, in the case of international students, the difficulty of getting to know home students.

These early baseline surveys showed that we had our work cut out! While a sense of belonging to the institution as a whole is to be valued, assessment and learning requirements, expectations and standards reside at disciplinary and programme level. It was the discipline and programme, then, that became the focus of our endeavours.

4.3 Methods of cultivating community

4.3.1 Provision of affinity space

We focussed on the physical in enhancing opportunities for dialogue and collaboration within the undergraduate Business programmes at Brookes by pioneering the design and construction of 'affinity space' (or space in which informal learning takes place (Gee 2004)) on our satellite campus. We aimed to provide students and staff with a much-needed physical space that would support both social learning and informal, impromptu student/student and student/staff interaction. The design of learning spaces is now acknowledged as having a powerful impact on student learning, engagement and assessed performance (Kuh et al. 2005). In the US, for example, those students who are taught together are also grouped together in residences, with those residences additionally being used for teaching and learning purposes, which strengthens cohort identity and fosters student peer support (Edwards and Sweeton 2000).

The physical environment of Britain's oldest universities, Oxford and Cambridge, encapsulates the concept of community. A college system characterised physically by central quads and cloistered walks allows communities to live and work together in a relatively secure environment. Post-1992 universities are not so lucky—their legacy usually involves a mixed bag of functional spaces with few, if any, intentionally designed spaces to facilitate social learning and informal interaction. Recently in the UK, however, interest in social learning spaces (spaces that can be used for both social and learning activities, supported by facilitative technology (Chism 2006)) has grown. Our work has informed and influenced some of the resulting development. Initially we part-funded renovation, and carried out a pilot colonisation study, of a small social learning space on a satellite campus (Greenwood et al. 2006). Then (after further extensive research and visits to other such spaces in the UK: the Saltaire Centre at Glasgow Caledonian University and the Learning Grid at Warwick University, for example) we used our capital funding as a Centre for Excellence in Teaching and Learning to design and construct a new building, a social learning space—the Simon Williams Undergraduate Centre. This building combines café facilities, technology (PCs, smart boards, interactive white boards, video recording facilities), flexible furnishings and support staff offices and is specifically designed to support both formal collaborative work between students and opportunities for informal interactions between students and staff.

This combination of facilities not only supports social learning, but also 'tunes into' the behaviours of the current generation of students. In the past students' learning behaviours were individual and sequential, involving research in a quiet library, followed by writing up of an assignment by oneself, interspersed by defined refreshment breaks taken in the student refectory with friends. The academic and the social were separate entities. In the 2000s, however, learning and social behaviours have become merged (Lomas and Oblinger 2006). Today's students use Wi-Fi connectivity to research and collaborate on assignments in cafés, halls of residence and even bars (9% of the 488 students in our early surveys declared that they frequently met in local pubs to do assessed group work). They favour places in which they can eat and drink, word-processing their work as they go, all the while communicating with others via email and mobile phone.

Once the Simon Williams Undergraduate Centre was open, we were interested in understanding how it was being colonised, why it was being colonised in this way, and the preferences of its users. We therefore conducted a colonisation study during the first two years of the building's occupation. Data was collected via online surveys, short face-to-face surveys and 'mental mapping exercises' with students. Semi-structured interviews and focus groups were also conducted with both staff and students, and a group of undergraduate student researchers recorded colonisation and use of the building four times daily for an academic year. Key findings from these various surveys revealed the importance of: locating social learning spaces along main movement corridors of a campus to promote informal interaction; ensuring connectivity with the rest of the campus environment via clear connections with other spaces, both indoor and outdoor; the presence of natural light, flexible furniture and food and drink; and providing an internal layout that allows students to both see and be seen but that also offers places of refuge where students can tuck themselves away.[1] Prior research also suggests that spaces are more successful when they have a strong sense of identity—and the interior decoration and ambience of the Simon Williams Undergraduate Centre was in fact selected by students themselves. A design company put together a series of 'mood boards' depicting different styles of interior decor and students voted for their preferred style over the period of a week.

The Simon Williams Undergraduate Centre has been robustly colonised by students and staff—students work both collaboratively and individually in the building, making use of the technology and refreshment facilities, while staff use the space for their own collaborative meetings and to socialise, eat and drink. However, our one disappointment has been that there is little informal interaction between staff and students, with students voicing trepidation at the prospect of approaching staff in the building (Kiddle 2009). Arguably, then, such physical affinity space enhanced dialogue and collaboration and indeed a sense of community—but within separate and distinct staff and student groupings. Affinity space provides the opportunity for informal interactions and dialogue between students and staff but something more—something intentional—is required to transform that opportunity into a reality and foster a community of assessment practice.

[1] See Kiddle (2009) for a comprehensive report on the colonisation study of the building and its findings.

4.3.2 Provision of formal and informal opportunities for dialogue and interaction

In addition to focussing on the physical as a means of cultivating a sense of community, we also focus on social, interactive aspects of learning, both formal and informal. Our intention is to enhance student involvement and participation in a community of assessment practice via (a) central, classroom-based assessment and feedback practices, (b) formal learning and assessment practices outside the classroom, and (c) opportunities to participate in informal activities outside the classroom.

Participation in formal classroom-based assessment and feedback practices

As we have seen in earlier chapters, some traditional assessment practices isolate and segregate the assessed from the assessor: students write an essay, submit it, and wait to hear back from an unknown marker to whom they may be anonymous. However, in Chapter 2, we introduced our social constructivist process model of assessment, by which students become joint partners (with staff) in learning, actively engaged with every stage in the assessment process in order to truly understand the complex and often tacit requirements of assessment. Chapters 4, 5, and 6 built on this theoretical model by setting out practical ways in which student participation can be enhanced at three stages in the assessment process: pre-assessment; during the act of assessment itself; and post-assessment (during feedback).

Pre-assessment, we have shown our intervention (discussed in detail in Chapter 4) to be highly effective in actively engaging learners with assessment standards and criteria, which leads to enhanced understanding and improved performance over the long term. Later on, such 'seasoned' students can participate more fully in self-assessment and peer assessment activities (including peer review and dialogue), applying their knowledge of standards and criteria and becoming assessors themselves. In some Business modules, second and third year students are asked to take part in assessment panels of first-year student presentations. We have also introduced, across the Business School, face-to-face feedback sessions in which individuals or small groups of students engage in oral feedback dialogue with their tutors.

In these ways, we are aiming to cultivate, through intentional and formal methods, a community of practice in which students actively engage with their tutors and peers over the process of assessment. That students should play a significant part in evaluative feedback of their own and others' learning, and be encouraged to engage in dialogue about their learning with tutors, clearly constitutes a more participatory, less hierarchical assessment process, in which the traditional, rigid divide between assessed and assessor begins to soften.

Participation in formal assessment and learning practices outside the classroom

There are a number of ways in which we have enhanced students' participation in formal assessment practices outside the classroom, and these have typically involved students holding defined roles which support learning and assessment activities.

At the Business School we have run Peer Assisted Learning (PAL) for many years whereby students who have successfully taken a module in the past facilitate the learning of current students via optional, drop-in sessions. PAL leaders are trained in facilitation techniques, and published evaluation of the process (Price and Rust 1995) demonstrates its benefits, both for leaders and participants. Unsurprisingly, most students choose to drop in during the weeks running up to their assessment deadlines.

Between 2005 and 2010, we extended such participatory roles to involve more students and a greater ability range. One of the most successful new roles is that of module assistant which, unlike the PAL leader, is not a student-facing role, but involves course administration. Staff who lead modules with over 100 students (and there are many such modules within the Business School) have the opportunity to employ a student assistant. These students work in partnership with module leaders to manage the delivery of modules, engaging in many activities such as organising learning materials, monitoring attendance and analysing module evaluations, to name but a few. These partnerships achieve a range of useful outcomes. Students, by working in tandem with staff, come to more fully understand the rationale underlying learning and assessment structures and processes. By becoming joint partners in the organisational learning process, they and their module leaders endeavour, together, to deliver worthwhile learning experiences. Module leaders and module assistants engage in dialogue not just about the work at hand but also about their broader experiences of being an academic or a student. This new, shared understanding ripples out to peers and colleagues alike.

Other innovative roles have involved students in pedagogic research, either as research assistants (see the colonisation study described in section 4.3.1 above), or via engagement in longitudinal research on the student learning experience. In the latter example, students were given the opportunity to become 'audio diarists', whereby they recorded short (10-15 minute) weekly audio commentaries on their student experience. The resulting insights were wide-ranging and enabled us to come to know in more detail the lived student experience including, for example, assessment pressure points, students' thirst for more personalised learning, and the influence of outside pressures on academic performance (Morosanu, Handley and O'Donovan 2010).

Another new role, that of technical assistant, is linked to our affinity space and involves technically skilled students facilitating other students' use of learning technologies within the Simon Williams Undergraduate Centre, as well as assisting with more general undergraduate support services, such as return of coursework.

These formal, defined roles provide opportunities for students to engage in an academic community of practice outside the classroom. They break down barriers and strengthen relationships between students and staff by engaging them in joint ventures with shared goals, thereby increasing students' confidence when speaking to and interacting with staff, as well as increasing staff understanding of the student experience. These roles provide a starting point for dialogue and also allow students to gain a greater understanding of assessment and learning processes in general as well as (in some cases) enabling them to share their understanding with their peers, who in turn become more engaged, assessment literate members of the community of practice.

Participation in informal activities outside the classroom

The final focus of our efforts to enhance student participation and cultivate staff and student interaction has been less formal, largely social activities. The following list is by no means exhaustive or prescriptive, but simply represents a small number of overlapping initiatives that we have tried within the Business School. Furthermore, as stressed throughout this book, cultivating both sense of community and a community of assessment practice are long-term aspirations and we are not in a position to make any grand claims to success after only a few years' work. Examples of initiatives that we have tried include:

- Staff supporting and mentoring leaders of student societies by providing them with a little seed money and assisting them in negotiation of university procedures.

- Organising an annual 'carnival' reception to welcome new students on campus, which combines both the academic and the social. Students are able to meet their personal tutors and also to enjoy barbeque food, the sounds of the samba and the vision of talented street performers—both students and professionals.

- Encouraging, supporting and part funding programmes in the organisation of combined staff and student events such as Chinese New Year festivities, photography competitions and boat trips.

- Providing expertise to support student groups in devising and staging events. In one first-year module students put together plans for events that are aimed at encouraging valuable peer and staff interaction and community participation. Those groups producing the most feasible and successful event plans are then given the opportunity to stage their events the following year, with funds made available to provide a financial safety net in case the events fail to break even. This allows the students involved to reflect on both their experience and the event outcomes.

These kinds of activities encourage students to become involved in the academic community in various ways. They cut across both the academic and the social and they provide informal opportunities for students and staff to interact and engage with one another. By focusing on informal, non-classroom-based activities we hope to cultivate a community in which students and staff feel more comfortable in one another's company and in which there is a less rigid student/staff divide. This will lead in turn, we hope, to a community of practice in which students and staff engage in dialogue about learning and assessment practice, as well as engaging at a social level.

4.4 Links with assessment literacy

New students do not immediately appreciate the benefits of developing self-evaluative abilities in order to make informed judgements about their own work and that of their peers. Indeed, many tend to hold an absolute view of the nature of knowledge and learning, believing in knowledge as certainty, answers as right or wrong, and a clear divide between teacher and student (Perry 1970). Such assessment illiterate students are unlikely to make effective PAL leaders or be able to evaluate modules effectively. In order to become active and effective learning partners, students need to be able to make informed evaluations not only of their own and their peers' learning, but also of the learning environment including the teaching. In order to do this, they need to become assessment literate.

In the US, formal pedagogic courses on learning have improved the quantity and quality of student contribution (Hutchings 2005)—these courses have improved students' pedagogic and assessment literacy. However, most programmes in the UK have little room for a purpose built course or module on pedagogy. Clearly, the assessment interventions that we discussed in Chapter 4 and the feedback practices that we described in Chapter 6 go some way towards orientating students in the assessment practices of the community. We have seen that marking practice, peer review and dialogic feedback all build assessment literacy. However, we believe that, for maximum efficacy, such processes must be intentional, coherent and recurrent. One lone peer review experience is unlikely to build complete and lasting assessment literacy. What is required is a programme approach (such as that which we described in Chapter 3) in which programme-wide assessment interventions are developed and applied at appropriate points in the programme by assessment literate staff. For students participating in such coordinated activities at programme level, their assessment literacy will be enhanced, and the community of practice itself will also become stronger by dint of these very activities and experiences which its members (both students and staff) share. Oxford Brookes University is already moving in this direction, having adopted and embedded into its policy our Assessment Compact[2] which tasks all university programmes with developing assessment literacy and co-ordinating assessment tasks across modules.

5. Conclusion

The literature tells us that community plays a key role in engaging students and enhancing their learning, yet it contains few practical examples of how to cultivate a sense of community, or indeed a community of practice. In this chapter we have aimed to redress the balance by sharing our own experiences in the Business School at Oxford Brookes University. It is clear that community is a complex concept and that many factors may be relevant to the success of a community. Consequently, we have tackled the issue of its cultivation on a number of fronts—physical, social, formal learning in the classroom, informal learning outside the classroom. We have seen that on each front, inroads can be made, and we can begin to cultivate a community of practice, but no one front appears to be dominant—it is likely, then, that a combination of interrelated factors (physical, social and pedagogic) will contribute to the success or otherwise of a community of assessment practice. Classroom-based interventions such as our assessment intervention play some part in developing students' assessment literacy, but in order to achieve full impact they need to be grounded within a learning environment in which student participation is sought and enhanced across a number of wide-ranging activities. It is also apparent that in higher education institutions (as they currently stand in the UK at least), some kind of deliberate

---

[2] Available at: http://www.brookes.ac.uk/aske/BrookesACompact/.

initiative is often required in order to kick start the process of interaction amongst students and staff which is a prerequisite for the development of a community of assessment practice. That community will not simply develop by itself, in the absence of intentional action.

Conclusion

To operate successfully within the assessment environments of their institutions both staff and students have always had to learn the assessment rules and systems, often largely through trial and error. For staff there has been an expectation that they would swiftly internalise and accept the norms and standards of their colleagues, including the workings of assessment. However, in practice, assessment literacy has often developed only gradually in a serendipitous if not idiosyncratic way and consequently has often remained largely underdeveloped. Students have long been focused on navigating the rules and working out the proclivities and preferences of individual staff, and only very gradually gain an understanding of the system that is critical to their final results. The idea that students should be encouraged and even supported to be assessment literate is only just receiving recognition, and consequently the means to support this development is in its infancy.

Within this book we have endeavoured to (1) conceptualise 'assessment literacy' in relation to the roles of staff and students; (2) identify and analyse its main components; and (3) provide practical guidance for its development among staff and students.

Chapter 1 focussed on defining assessment literacy. We learnt that assessment literacy is a gateway or threshold concept. Staff are expected to have a basic level of assessment literacy in order to take responsibility for assessment. For students, being assessment literate enables them to engage with assessment standards at a deep level, to understand the nature and purpose of assessment tasks, and to select appropriate approaches to them, thereby performing more effectively when undertaking assessed tasks. Assessment literacy encompasses both technical and conceptual understanding but at its heart, as shown in Chapter 2's theoretical approach, is the need for a holistic approach to assessment and the centrality of a relational dynamic and dialogue between staff and student.

A foundation for this approach is an understanding of the nature of assessment standards which is therefore identified within the definition as a key component of assessment literacy. Without an understanding of assessment standards and how they are used in professional holistic judgement some other aspects of assessment literacy cannot be developed (e.g. self- and peer assessment). Consequently how that understanding of assessment standards is developed is the focus of Chapter 2. This chapter culminated in our proposal of a 'cultivated community of practice' model which acknowledges that, through mutual engagement and a shared repertoire of resources in the joint endeavour of assessment, staff and students become increasingly assessment literate.

The role and importance of the community of practice was further explored in Chapter 7. This chapter attempted to explain and evidence why a community focus is important to students' academic performance. Within a case study approach this chapter also explored practical ways in which a sense of community and a community of practice can be cultivated, drawn from our experience of the initiatives that we have seeded in the Business School at Oxford Brookes University.

Practical and evidence-based guidance for the development of assessment literacy was largely provided in Chapters 3 to 6 where each looked at a separate stage of the assessment process:

Chapter 3 focussed on the planning of assessment. The key message of this chapter was the importance of adopting a programme-wide approach to the design of assessment, as opposed to a module-focused approach, which is currently much more common in universities around the world. Only by adopting a programme-wide approach can we adequately measure the achievement of programme outcomes and take into account slowly-learnt literacies and complex learning. This chapter also provided some concrete suggestions of the kinds of factors that need to be considered, and the decisions that need to be made, when planning a programme-level assessment strategy.

In Chapter 4, we concentrated on students and looked at pre-assessment activity—or the kinds of techniques and exercises that staff can use to prepare their students for assessment, to increase their assessment literacy, and to improve their learning. We detailed our own widely adopted assessment intervention—which improves student learning by developing student understanding of assessment criteria and processes via a marking exercise and workshop discussion—as well as exploring other, smaller studies and interventions. The evidence set out in this chapter showed that students who are engaged in activities that involve them thinking about, discussing and applying the assessment criteria come to a fuller understanding of those criteria sooner. This enables them to perform better when undertaking assessed work. The key aims of this chapter were (a) to illustrate the importance and value of students taking part in pre-assessment activity; and (b) to explain how staff can implement such activity, even in an environment of large student numbers and scant resources by using an assessment intervention similar to our own.

Chapter 5 concentrated on assessment activities. For students, if they are assessment literate, they can make judgements about the quality of their work while they are working on the assessment tasks and need not wait for post-assessment feedback to have an idea about its quality. So techniques such as peer review, self-assessment and providing feedback on drafts during assessment preparation should support students to learn self regulation. However staff's role in assessment activity was the main focus of this chapter, in particular the assessment tasks that staff choose to set for their students; and marking. In terms of choice of assessment task, we examined the kinds of considerations that staff will need to take into account when deciding on assessment tasks, and the types of constraint that they may meet. In terms of marking student work, we examined both the criterion-referenced and the norm-referenced approach, identifying deep inadequacies with both approaches, and introducing our own community-of-practice-based approach to marking as a more objective and reliable alternative. The key message of this chapter was that staff do not undertake assessment activity in a vacuum. They are constrained and influenced by factors such as the institutional and the programme environment, the manageability of assessment tasks, and the necessity of providing adequate feedback. Furthermore—and most importantly—staff and assessors work within a community of academic and assessment practice, and academic standards reside in this community of practice. It is through immersion in the community that staff come to know the local assessment practices, standards and criteria fully and are able to apply them consistently.

The focus of Chapter 6 was post-assessment activity, largely the production and use of end-of-assessment feedback. Its key message was that feedback, whether provided during preparation of assessed work or after completion, plays a fundamental role in developing student assessment literacy and, more generally, is fundamental to student learning. We examined why so many students have negative experiences of feedback and we provided some practical examples of how feedback can be improved in order to heighten student engagement with feedback and to improve its efficacy. We also introduced our own analytical stages of engagement model, which depicts the various stages of engagement within the feedback process and highlights points of, and reasons for, students' disengagement from feedback.

And so we have reached the end of this book, but we are not at the end of our journey. The key message is that for dissatisfaction with assessment to be addressed and for assessment to become effective (and efficient) staff and students need to become assessment literate. The importance assessment literacy is accorded and the resources allocated to its development will reflect the culture and priorities of each institution. Those institutions with assessment literate staff will recognise the importance of community and dialogue, and should be in a better position to support their students. And the basic underlying enabler of assessment literacy (for both staff and students) is community. After all, it is very difficult to plan an effective programme-wide approach to assessment; or to engage students in pre-assessment activity; or to design effective assessment tasks; or to mark consistently and fairly; or to provide meaningful, engaging feedback in the absence of a supportive and inclusive community of academic practice whose members interact and share an understanding of the role and nature of assessment. Throughout this book we have set out the evidence in support of the fundamental role that community plays in the development of assessment literacy. However there is still much work required to understand how this literacy can be effectively developed and there are many practices beyond those described in the book that make a contribution but are not widespread. So if students are to reach their potential in terms of their assessed performance and to live up to the expectations of being proficient evaluators of their education and the service they receive, we must be proactive in supporting them to develop the skills and understanding, the assessment literacy, that they need to make a useful and constructive contribution in shaping their educational experience and to maximise their learning.

Bibliography

(2009). *National Student Forum Annual Report 2009*:
www.nationalstudentforum.com.

Alverno College Faculty. (1994). *Student Assessment-as-Learning at Alverno College*.
Milwaukee, WI: Alverno College Institute.

Askew, S. and Lodge, C. (2000). Gifts, ping-pong and loops—linking feedback and
learning. In S. Askew (ed.), *Feedback for Learning*. London: Routledge.

Astin, A. W. (1993). *What Matters in College: Four Critical Years Revisited*. San
Francisco: Jossey-Bass.

Astin, A.W. (1984). Student involvement: A developmental theory for higher
education. *Journal of College Student Personnel 25*, 297-308.

Baird, J.-A. (2010). Beliefs and practice in teacher assessment. *Assessment in
Education: Principles, Policy & Practice 17(1)*, 1-5.

Baume, C. and Baume, D. (1992). *Course Design for Active Learning. Effective
Learning and Teaching in Higher Education, Module 2, Parts 1 & 2*. Sheffield: CVCP
Universities' Staff Devlopment and Training Unit.

Baxter, Magolda, M. B. (1992). *Knowing and Reasoning in College: Gender-Related
Patterns in Students' Intellectual Development*. San Francisco: Jossey-Bass.

Baxter Magolda, M. B. and King, P. M. (2004). *Learning Partnerships: Theories and
Models of Practice to Educate for Self-Authorship*. Sterling, VA: Stylus.

Becket, N. and Brookes, M. (Autumn 2009). More than just a name and a number!
Strategies to personalise the student learning experience. *Teaching News*.

Biggs, J. (1999). *Teaching for Quality Learning at University*. Buckingham: SRHE and
Open University Press.

Black, P., Harrison, C., Hodgen, H., Marshall, B. and Serret, N. (2010). Validity in teachers' summative assessments. *Assessment in Education: Principles, Policy & Practice 17(2)*, 215-32.

Bloom, B. (May 1968). Comment, *UCLA CSEIP Evaluation 1(2)*.

Bloom, B. S. (1956). Taxonomy of educational objectives: the classification of educational goals. In B. S. Bloom, *Handbook 1. Cognitive Domain*. New York: David McKay.

Bloxham, S. and Boyd, P. (2011). Accountability in grading student work: securing academic standards in a 21st century quality assurance context. *British Educational Research Journal*, iFirst Article, 1-20.

Bloxham, S. and Boyd, P. (2007). *Developing Effective Assessment in Higher Education: A Practical Guide*. Maidenhead: Open University Press.

Bloxham, S. Boyd, P. and Orr, S. (2011). Mark my words: the role of assessment criteria in UK higher education grading practices. *Studies in Higher Education 36(6)*, 655-70.

Bloxham, S. and West, A. (2007). Learning to write in higher education: students' perceptions of an intervention in developing undrestanding of assessment criteria. *Teaching in Higher Education 12(1)*, 77-89.

Bloxham, S. and West, A. (2004). Understanding the rules of the game: marking peer assessment as a medium for developing students' conceptions of assessment. *Assessment and Evaluation in Higher Education 29(6)*, 721-33.

Boud, D. (29-31 May 2007). Great designs: what should assessment do? REAP International Online Conference on Assessment Design for Learner Responsibility: http://ewds.strath.ac.uk/REAP07.

Boud, D. (2000). Sustainable assessment: rethinking assessment for the learning society. *Studies in Continuing Education 22(2)*, 151-67.

Boud, D. and Falchikov, N. (2007). *Rethinking Assessment in Higher Education: Learning for the Longer Term*. Abingdon: Rouledge.

Bradford, Univ. of (2009). *Programme Assessment Strategies (PASS)*: http://www.pass.brad.ac.uk/.

Bridges, P. and Bourdillon, P. (1999). Discipline related marking behaviour using percentages: a potential cause of inequity in assessment. *Assessment & Evaluation in Higher Education 24(3)*, 285-301.

Brookes M. and Beckett, N. (2011). The internationalisation of hospitality management degree programmes. *International Journal of Contemporary Hospitality Management 23(2)*, 241-69.

Brown, E. and Glover, C. (2006). Evaluating written feedback. In C. Bryan (ed.), *Innovative Assessment in Higher Education* (pp. 81-91). Abingdon: Routledge.

Brown, S. and Knight, P. (1994). *Assessing Learners in Higher Education*. London: Kogan Page.

Burgess, R. (2007). *Beyond the Honours Degree Classification: Burgess Group Final Report*. Universities UK.

Butler, R. (1988). Enhancing and undermining intrinsic motivation. *British Journal of Educational Psychology 58*, 1-14.

Butler, R. (1987). Task-involving and ego-involving properties of evaluation. *Journal of Educational Psychology 79*, 474-82.

Chinn, C. A. and Brewer, W. F. (1993). The role of anomalous data in knowledge acquisition: a theoretical framework and implications for science instruction. *Review of Educational Research 63*, 1-49.

Chism, N. V. (2006). Challenging traditional assumptions and rethinking learning spaces. In D. G. Oblinger (ed.), *Learning Spaces*. USA: Educause.

Donald, J. G. (2009). The commons: disciplinary and interdisciplinary encounters. In C. Kreber (ed.), *The University and its Disciplines*. New York: Routledge.

Ecclestone, K. (2001). 'I know a 2:1 when I see it': Understanding criteria for degree classification in franchised university programmes. *Journal of Further and Higher Education 25*, 301-313.

Edwards, K. and Sweeton, N. (2000). Learning communities: past, present and future. *Journal of Student Affairs 9*, 42-51.

Eljamal, M. B., Arnold, G. L. and Sharp, S. (1999). Intellectual development: a complex teaching goal. *Studies in Higher Education 24(1)*, 7-25.

Elton, L. (1997). 'Is University Teaching Researchable?' Inaugural Lecture, University College London.

Falchikov, N. (2005). *Improving Assessment through Student Involvement*. Abingdon: RoutledegeFalmer.

Forbes, D. A. and Spence, J. (1991). An experiment in assessment for a large class. In R. Smith (ed.), *Innovations in Engineering Education*. London: Ellis Horwood.

Freeman, R. and Lewis, R. (1998). *Planning and Implementing Assessment*. London: Kogan Page.

Fritz, C. O. et al. (2000). When further learning fails: stability and change following repeated presentation of text. *British Journal of Psyhology 91*, 493-511.

Gee, J. P. (2004). *Situated Language and Learning: A Critique of Traditional Schooling.* London: Routledge.

Gibbs, G. and Coffey, M. (2004). The impact of training of university teachers on their teaching skills, their approach to teaching and the approach to learning of their students. *Active Learning in Higher Education 5(1)*, 87-100.

Gibbs, G. and Dunbar-Goddet, H. (2007). *The Effects of Programme Assessment Environments on Student Learning.* York: Higher Education Academy: http://www.heacademy.ac.uk/assets/York/documents/ourwork/research/gibbs_050 6.pdf.

Gibbs, G., Knapper, C. and Piccinin, S. (2009). *Departmental Leadership in Research-Intensive Environments.* Leadership Foundation in Higher Education Research and Development Series: http://www.heacademy.ac.uk/assets/EvidenceNet/gibbs.pdf.

Gibbs, G., Knapper, C. and Picinnin, S. (2007). *Departmental Leadership for Quality Teaching: An International Comparative Study of Effective Practice.* The Higher Education Academy. Summary only available at: http://www.heacademy.ac.uk/assets/York/documents/ourwork/EvidenceNet/Summ aries/gibbsg_et_al_departmental_leadership_for_quality_teaching_summary.pdf.

Gibbs, G. and Simpson, C. (2004). Conditions under which assessment supports students' learning. *Learning and Teaching in Higher Education 1(1)*, 1-31.

Gibbs, P., Angelides, P. and Michaelides, P. (2004). Preliminary thoughts on a praxis of higher education teaching. *Teaching in Higher Education 9*, 183-94.

Gillet, A. and Hammond, A. (2009). Mapping the maze of assessment: an investigation into practice. *Active Learning in Higher Education 10(2)*, 120-37.

Greeno, J. G., Collins, A. M., and Resnick, L. B. (1996). Cognition and Learning. In D. A. Berliner, *Handbook of Educational Psychology* (pp. 15-41). New York: Macmillan.

Greenwood, M., O'Donovan, B. and Rust, C. (2006). 'A small-scale experiment in the development of social-learning space.' Presented at the Second Symposium on Social Learning Space, Warwick, UK.

Gusfiled, J. R. (1975). *The Community: A Critical Response.* New York: Harper Colophon.

Handley, K., Den Outer, B. and Price, M. (2012). Learning to mark: exemplars, dialogue and participation in assessment communities. *Higher Education Research and Development*, January.

Handley, K. Price, M. and Millar, J. (June 2008). *Engaging Students with Assessment Feedback: Final Report for the FDTL5 Project 144/03*. Business School, Oxford Brookes University.

Hattie, J. and Timperley, H. (2007). The power of feedback. *Review of Educational Research 77(1)*, 81-112.

Havnes, A. (2008). 'There's another story behind.' Presented at the Fourth Biennual Northumbra/EARL SIG Assessement Conference, Potsdam, Berlin, 27-29 August.

Havnes, A. (2007). 'What can feedback practices tell us about variation in grading across fields?' Presented at the ASKe Seminar Series, Oxford Brookes University, 19 September.

Havnes, A. and McDowell, L. (eds) 2008. Introduction in *Balancing Dilemmas in Assessment and Learning in Contemporary Education*. London: Routledge.

Higgins, R. (2000). 'Be more critical!: rethinking assessment feedback.' Presented at the British Educational Research Association Conference. Available at http://www.leeds.ac.uk/educol/documents/00001548.htm.

Higgins, R., Hartley, P. and Skelton, A. (2002). The conscientious consumer; reconsidering the role of assessment feedback in student learning. *Studies in Higher Education 27(1)*, 53-64.

Holmes, L., and Smith, L. (July/August 2003). Student evaluation of faculty grading methods. *Journal of Education for Business*, 318-23.

Hornby, W. (2003). Assessing using grade-related criteria: a single currency for universities? *Assessment & Evaluation in Higher Education 28(4)*, 435-54.

Hounsell, D. (1987). Essay writing and the quality of feedback. In J. T.-P. Richardson (ed.), *Student Learning: Research in Education and Cognitive Psychology*. Milton Keynes: SRHE & Open University.

Hudson, J. (20 May 2010). *Programme-Level Assessment: A Review of Selected Material*. Report prepared for the Bradford NTF PASS Team.

Hughes, I. E. (1995). Peer assessment. *Capability 30(1)*, 39-43.

Hutchings, P. (2005). *Building Pedagogical Intelligence*. Carnegie Perspectives: http://www.carnegiefoundation.org/perspectives/.

Hyland, P. (2000). Learning from feedback on assessment. In P. A. Hyland, *The Practice of University History Teaching* (pp. 233-47). Manchester: Manchester University Press.

Juwah, C., Macfarlane-Dick, D., Matthew, R., Nicol, D., Ross, D. and Smith, B. (2004). *Enhancing Student Learning through Effective Formative Feedback*. The Higher Education Academy: http://www.heacademy.ac.uk/resources.

Kiddle, R. (2009). *Colonisation Study: The Design of the Simon Williams Undergraduate Building: Wheatley Campus: Oxford Brookes University*. Available at: http://www.brookes.ac.uk/aske/documents/Kiddle%202009%20Brookes%20SWUC %20Colonisation%20Study.pdf.

King, P. M. and Kitchener, K. S. (1994). *Developing Reflective Judgement*. San Francisco: Jossey-Bass.

Klenowski, V., Askew, S. and Carnell, E. (2006). Portfolios for learning, assessment and professional development in higher education. *Assessment and Evaluation in Higher Education 31(3)*, 267-86.

Knight, P. T. (2002). Summative assessment in higher education: practices in disarray. *Studies in Higher Education 27(4)*, 275-86.

Knight, P. T. (2001). Complexity and curriculum: a process approach to curriculum-making. *Teaching in Higher Education 6(3)*, 369-81.

Knight, P. T. (2000). The value of a programme-wide approach to assessment. *Assessment and Evaluation in Higher Education 25(3)*, 237-51.

Knight, P. T. and Mantz, Y. (2004). *Learning, Curriculum and Employability in Higher Education*. London: Routledge.

Knight, P. T. and Yorke, M. (2003). *Assessment, Learning and Employability*. Maidenhead: SRHE and Open University Press.

Kolb, D. A. (1984). *Experiential Learning: Experience as the Source of Learning and Development*. New Jersey: Prentice-Hall.

Kuh, G. D., Kinzie, J., Schuh, J. H., Whitt, E. J. and Associates. (2005). *Student Success in College: Creating Conditions that Matter*. San Francisco: Jossey-Bass.

Laming, D. (2004) *Human Judgement: The Eye of the Beholder*. London: Thomson.

Laurillard, D. (1993). *Rethinking University Teaching: A Framework for the Effective Use of Educational Technology*. London: Routledge.

Lave, J. and Wenger, E. (1991). *Situated Learning. Legitimate Peripheral Participation*. Cambridge: University of Cambridge Press.

Lea, M. and Street, B. (1998). Student writing in higher education: an academic literacies approach. *Studies in Higher Education, 23*, 157-72.

Lomas, C. and Oblinger, D. G. (2006). Student practices and their impact on learning spaces. In D. G. Oblinger (ed.), *Learning Spaces*. USA: Educause.

Maclellan, E. (2001). Assessment for learning, the different perceptions of tutors and students. *Assessment and Evaluation in Higher Education 26(4)*, 307-18.

Mann, S. (2001). Alternative perspectives on the student experience: alienation and engagement. *Studies in Higher Education 26(1)*, 7-19.

McCulloch, A. (2009). The student as co-producer: learning from public administration about the student–university relationship. *Studies in Higher Education 34(2)*, 171-83.

McDonald, B. and Boud, D. (2003). The impact of self-assessment on achievement: the effects of self-assessment training on performance in external examinations. *Assessment in Education 10(2)*, 209-20.

Meyer, J. H. and Land, R. (2006). *Overcoming Barriers to Student Understanding: Threshold Concepts and Troublesome Knowledge*. Abingdon, New York: Routledge.

Miller, C. M. I. and Parlett, M. (1974). *Up to the Mark: a Study of the Examination Game*. Guildford: Society for Research into Higher Education.

Morosanu, L., Handley, K. and O'Donovan, B. (2010). Seeking support: researching first-year students' experience of coping with academic life. *Higher Education Research & Development 29(6)*, 665–78.

Nelson, C. E. (1994). Critical thinking and collaborative learning. In K. A. Bosworth, *Collaborative Learning and College Teaching*. San Francisco, CA: Jossey-Bass.

Newman, M. (2009). NSS targeted in linguistics battle. *Times Higher Education*, 14 May.

Nicol, D. J. and Macfarlane-Dick, D. (2006). Formative assessment and self-regulated learning: a model and seven principles of good feedback practice. *Studies in Higher Education 31(2)*, 199-218.

Nicol, D. J. and Macfarlane-Dick, D. (2004). *Rethinking Formative Assessment in HE: A Theoretical Model and Seven Principles of Good Feedback Practice*. Available at: www.heacademy.ac.uk/assets/York/documents/ourwork/tla/assessment/web0015_r ethinking_formative_assessment_in_he.pdf.

Nonaka, I. (1991). The knowledge-creating company. *The Harvard Business Review*, November-December, 96-104.

Northedge, A. (2003a). Enabling participation in academic discourse. *Teaching in Higher Education 8(2)*, 169-80.

Northedge, A. (2003b). Rethinking teaching in the context of diversity. *Teaching in Higher Education 8(1)*, 17-32.

Northedge, A. (2002). Organizing excursions into specialist discourse communities: a sociocultural account of university teaching. In G. Wells and G. Claxton, *Learning for Life in the 21st Century. Sociocultural Perspectives on the Future of Education* (pp. 252-264). Oxford: Blackwell.

O'Donovan, B. and Price, M. (2007). Building community: engaging students within a disciplinary community of practice. Presented at the ISSOTL Conference, Sydney, Australia, July 2007.

O'Donovan, B., Price, M. and Rust, C. (2008). Developing student understanding of assessment standards: a nested hierarchy of approaches. *Teaching in Higher Education 13(2)*, 205-16.

O'Donovan, B., Price, M. and Rust, C. (2004). Know what I mean? Enhancing student understanding of assessment standards and criteria. *Teaching in Higher Education, 9(3)*, 325-35.

O'Donovan, B., Price, M. and Rust, C. (2000). The student experience of criterion-referenced assessment (through the introduction of a common criteria assessment grid). *Innovations in Education and Teaching International, 38(1)*, 74-85.

Orr, S. (2007). Assessment moderation: constructing the marks and constructing the students. *Assessment & Evaluation in Higher Education 32(6)*, 645-56.

Orsmond, P., Merry, S. and Callaghan, A. (2004). Implementation of a formative assessment model incorporating peer and self-assessment. *Innovations in Education and Teaching International 41(3)*, 273-90.

Orsmond, P., Merry, S. and Reiling, K. (2002). The use of exemplars and formative feedback when using student derived marking criteria in peer and self-assessment. *Assessment and Evaluation in Higher Education 27(4)*, 309-23.

Orsmond, P., Merry, S. and Reiling, K. (2000). The use of student derived marking criteria in peer and self assessment. *Assessment and Evaluation in Higher Education 25(1)*, 23-38.

Parker, J. (2002). A new disciplinarity: communities of knowledge, learning and practice. *Teaching in Higher Education, 7*, 373-86.

Perry, W. G. (1981). Cognitive and ethical growth: the making of meaning. In A. W. Chickering and Associates (eds), *The Modern American College: Responding to the New Realities of Diverse Students and a Changing Society* (pp. 76–116). San Francisco: Jossey-Bass.

Perry, W. G. (1970). *Forms of Intellectual and Ethical Development in the College Years: A Scheme*. New York: Holt, Rinehart and Winston.

Price, M. (1999). The experience of introducing a common criteria assessment grid across an academic department. *Quality in Higher Education, 5,* 133-144.

Price, M., Carroll, J. O'Donovan, B. and Rust, C. (2010). If I was going there, I wouldn't start from here—a critical commentary on current assessment practice. *Assessment and Evaluation in Higher Education 36(4),* 479-92.

Price, M. Handley, K. and Millar, J. (2011). Feedback—focussing attention on engagement. *Studies in Higher Education 36(8),* 879-96.

Price, M., Handley, K., Millar, J. and O'Donovan, B. (2010). Feedback: all that effort but what is the effect? *Assessment and Evaluation in Higher Education 35(3),* 277–89.

Price, M., O'Donovan, B. and Rust, C. (2007). Putting a social-constructivist assessment process model into practice: building the feedback loop into the assessment process through peer review. *Innovations in Education and Teaching International,* 44(2), 143-52.

Price, M. and Rust, C. (1995). Laying firm foundations: the long-term benefits of Supplemental Instruction for students on large introductory courses. *Innovations in Education and Training International 32(3),* 125-30.

QAA. (September 2006). *Code of Practice for the Assurance of Academic Quality and Standards in Higher Education, Section 6: Assessment of Students.*

Quinton, S. and Smallbone, T. (2010). Feeding forward: using feedback to promote student reflection and learning—a teaching model. *Innovations in Education & Teaching International 47(1),* 125-35.

Ramsden, P. (1992). *Learning to Teach in Higher Education.* London: Routledge.

Ridsdale, M. L. (2000) 'I've read his comments but I don't know how to do': International postgraduate student perceptions of written supervisor feedback. In K. Charnock (ed.) *Sources of Confusion: Refereed Proceedings of the National Language and Academic Skills Conference* (pp. 272-82). La Trobe University, 27-28 November.

Rotheram, B. (n.d.). *Sounds good: quicker, better assessment using audio feedback.* Available at: http://sites.google.com/site/soundsgooduk/.

Rovai, A. P. (2002). Development of an instrument to measure classroom community. *Internet and Higher Education 5(3),* 197-211.

Rovai, A. P. and Jordan, H. (2004). Blended learning and sense of community: a comparative analysis with traditional and fully online graduate courses. *The International Review of Research in Open and Distance Learning 5(2):* http://www.irrodl.org/index.php/irrodl/article/view/192/274.

Rust, C. (2011). The unscholarly use of numbers in our assessment practices: what will make us change? *International Journal for the Scholarship of Teaching and Learning 5(1)*.

Rust, C. (2007). Towards a scholarship of assessment (opinion piece). *Assessment and Evaluation in Higher Education 32(2)*, 229-37.

Rust, C. (2002). The impact of assessment on student learning: how can the research literature practically help to inform the development of departmental assessment strategies and learner-centred assessment practices? *Active Learning in Higher Education 3(2)*, 145-58.

Rust, C. (2001). *A Briefing on Assessment of Large Groups: LTSN Generic Centre Assessment Series No. 12*. York: LTSN.

Rust, C. (2000). A possible student-centred assessment solution to some of the current problems of modular degree programmes (opinion piece). *Active Learning in Higher Education 1(2)*, 126-31.

Rust, C., O'Donovan, B. and Price, M. (2005). A social constructivist assessment process model: how the research literature shows us this could be best practice. *Assessment and Evaluation in Higher Education, 30*, 231-40.

Rust, C., Price, M. and O'Donovan, B. (2003). Improving students' learning by developing their understanding of assessment criteria and processes. *Assessment and Evaluation in Higher Education, 28(2)*, 147-64.

Rust, C. and Smith, P. (2011). The potential of research-based learning for the creation of truly inclusive academic communities of practice. *Innovations in Education and Teaching International, 48(2)*, 115-25.

Sadler, D. (1987). Specifying and promulgating achievement standards. *Oxford Review of Education, 13*, 191-20.

Sadler, R. (2010). Close-range assessment practices with high-yield prospects. Keynote address at the EARLI/Northumbria Assessment Conference 2010. Northumberland, UK.

Sadler, R. (1989). Formative assessment and the design of instructional systems. *Instructional Science 18*, 119-144.

Sambell, K. (2010). Global theories and practices: institutional, disciplinary and cultural variations. Presented at the International Society for the Scholarship of Teaching and Learning (ISSOTL) Conference, Liverpool, 19-22 October.

Sastry, T. and Bekhradnia, B. (2007). *The Academic Experience of Students in English Universities*. Oxford: Higher Education Policy Institute.

Saunders, M. and Davis, S. (1998). The use of assessment criteria to ensure consistency of marking: some implications for good practice. *Quality Assurance in Higher Education, 6(3),* 162-71.

Savin Boden, M. and Howell Major, C. (2004). *Foundations of Problem Based Learning.* Maidenhead: Open University Press/SRHE.

Shute, V. L. (2008). Focus on formative feedback. *Review of Educational Research 78(1),* 153-89.

Skinner, B. F. (1968). *The Technology of Teaching.* New York: Appleton-Century-Crofts.

Snowdon, D. (2002). Complex acts of knowing: paradox and descriptive self-awareness. *Journal of Knowledge Management, 6,* 100-11.

Stobart, G. (2008). *Testing Times: The Uses and Abuses of Assessment.* Abingdon: Routledge.

Tan, K. (2007). Conceptions of self-assessment: what is needed for long-term learning? In D. A. Boud (ed.), *Rethinking Assessment in Higher Education: Learning for the Longer Term* (pp. 114-27). Abingdon: Routledge.

Taylor, S. M. (2011). Deeply embedded assessment conservatism and the loss of innocence: an accounting-based case study. Paper presented at the HERDSA 2011 Conference, Gold Coast, Queensland, 4-7 July.

Torrance, H. (1993). Formative assessment: some theoretical problems and empirical questions. *Cambridge Journal of Education 23(3),* 333-43.

Tsoukas, H. (2003). Do we really understand tacit knowledge? In Easterby-Smith, M. and Lyles, M. A. (eds), *The Blackwell Handbook of Organizational Learning and Knowledge Management.* Malden, MA; Oxford: Blackwell.

Vygotsky, L. (1978). *Mind in Society: The Development of Higher Psychological Processes.* MA: Harvard University Press.

Walker, M. (2009). An investigation into written comments on assignments: do students find them usable? *Assessment and Evaluation in Higher Education 34(1),* 67-78.

Webster, F. Pepper, D. and Jenkins, A. (2000). Assessing the undergraduate dissertation. *Assessment & Evaluation in Higher Education 25(1),* 71-80.

Wellman, B. and Wortley, S. (1990). Different strokes from different folks: community ties and social support. *American Journal of Sociology 96,* 558-88.

Wenger, E. (1998). *Communities of Practice: Learning, Meaning and Identity.* Cambridge: Cambridge University Press.

Wenger, E., McDermott, R. and Snyder, W. (2002). *Cultivating Communities of Practice*. Boston, MA: Harvard Business School Press.

Wiggins, G. (1993). *Assesssing Student Performance: Exploring the Purpose and Limits of Testing*. San Francisco: Jossey-Bass.

Winter, R. (2003). Contextualising the patchwork text: addressing problems of coursework assessment in higher education. *Innovations in Education and Teaching International 40(2)*, 112-22.

Winter, R. (1994). The problem of educational levels part 2: a new framework for credit accumulation in higher education. *Journal for Further and Higher Education, 18*, 92-107.

Wolf, A. (1997). *Assessment in Higher Education and the Role of 'Graduateness'*. London: Higher Education Quality Council.

Wotjas, O. (1998). Feedback? No, just give us the answers. *Times Higher Education Supplement*, 25 September.

Yorke, M. (2007). *Grading Student Achievement in Higher Education: Signals and Shortcomings*. London: Routledge.

Yorke, M. (2003). Formative assessment in higher education: moves towards theory and the enhancement of pedagogic practice. *Higher Education 45(4)*, 477-501.

Yorke, M. (2002). Subject benchmarking and the assessment of student learning. *Quality Assurance in Education 10(3)*, 155-71.

Yorke, M. (2001a). Formative assessment and its relevance to retention. *Higher Education Research and Development 20(2)*, 115-26.

Yorke, M. (2001b). Turn first-semester assessments into richer learning experiences. *Innovations in Education and Teaching International 38(3)*, 277-8.

Yorke, M. (1998). The management of assessment in higher education. *Assessment and Evaluation in Higher Education 23(2)*, 101-16.

Yorke, M., Bridges, P. and Wolfe, H. (2000). Mark distributions and marking practices in UK higher education. *Active Learning in Higher Education 1(1)*, 7-27.

Yorke, M. and Knight, P. T. (2006). Curricula for economic and social gain. *Higher Education 51(4)*, 565-88.

Index

A

academic standards 96-97, 100-101, 150

accumulative integrative project 58, 61

Achievement Matters 100

action 106, 108, 113, 122-128

affinity space 136-139, 142

allocation of resources 50

Alverno College 20

analytical stages of engagement model (feedback) 105, 122

assessment activity 45, 85-89, 91, 101, 104, 149, 150

assessment blocks 60

Assessment Compact 145

assessment criteria 10, 16, 17, 22, 32-42, 63-84, 92-94, 104, 107, 109-110, 116, 118, 149

assessment design 13, 14, 40, 46, 49, 58, 61-63

assessment illiterate 12, 14, 144

assessment intervention 22, 35-36, 63, 67, 74, 81, 83, 133, 145, 149

assessment literacy 7-16, 19, 20-24, 34-35, 44, 47, 56, 63-67, 72-76, 81-86, 101-107, 110-122, 127, 129, 131-135, 144-151

assessment standards 10, 17, 21-29, 32-37, 42-45, 75, 84, 86, 91-92, 96-99, 101, 106, 108, 111-112, 131, 133, 140, 147-148

assessor-like thinking 64

Astin 17, 43, 134-135

attention 110, 123-126, 128

B

Behaviourism 108

bell curve 89, 94-95

benchmark statements 29

benchmarking 100, 106, 108, 115

Bloom 11, 95

Bloxham 82, 86, 94, 96

Burgess Report 55

Business School (Oxford Brookes University) 29, 34, 38, 98, 136, 140-145, 148

C

camel 89, 95

capstone modules 47, 59

choice of assessment task 87, 149

cognitive engagement (feedback) 126, 127, 128

cognitivist (view of learning) 108

collection (feedback) 61

colonisation study 138-139, 142

community 18, 22, 73, 84, 86, 94, 97-101, 112, 118, 120, 128, 131-139, 140, 143-146, 148, 150-151

community of practice 22-26, 36, 37, 39, 40, 41-45, 66, 84, 86, 93, 90-99, 101, 104, 111-112, 116, 118-120, 126, 131-135, 141-142, 144-145, 148, 150

complex learning 12, 47-48, 61, 149

constructive alignment 87

constructively aligned 37, 38

criterion-referenced 38, 68, 91-94, 101, 104, 149

cue awareness 13

cultivated community of practice approach 44

cultivated community of practice model 23, 25-26, 37, 39, 40-45

cultivating academic community 133

cycle 26, 39, 40-42, 86, 106, 128

E

enabler 11, 150

engage 10, 13, 15, 21-22, 36-39, 41-42, 54, 59, 63, 83, 86, 88, 102, 110-118, 120-127, 132, 140-142, 144, 147, 151

engagement 10, 17, 19, 22, 25, 36-43, 54, 65, 83-86, 88, 97, 103, 105, 111-116, 119, 121-129, 132, 135, 137, 142, 148, 150

engagement with feedback 105, 112, 116, 122-125, 129, 150

exemplars 34, 64-67, 75-79, 81-84, 92, 116, 117, 120

expert 18, 28, 33, 35, 37, 42, 100, 108, 118

explicit model 24, 26, 28-33, 42

F

Falchikov 47, 104

FDLT 114

feedback 9-15, 18-19, 22-27, 30, 34, 38-42, 45, 47, 51-54, 61, 65, 68-69, 73, 77-79, 82, 85, 88-90, 94, 98, 102-129, 135, 140-141, 144, 149-151

feedback loop 89, 102, 108

forensic (role of feedback) 108, 110, 115

formative assessment 9, 47, 51-56, 61, 62, 87, 103

formative feedback 52-54, 61, 77, 79, 88, 89, 103, 106, 116

G

gateway 8-13, 21, 147

grid 29-35, 38, 68-70, 138

H

high-stakes assessment 54

HLST 99-100

I

improving feedback 113, 115, 123

independent learning 90

institutional context 48, 88

integrative assessment 59

intentionality 15

intervention 22, 34-36, 67-76, 80-84, 102-103, 133, 140, 145, 149

invisible criteria 72, 81

K

Kiddle 136, 139

Kolb (experiential learning cycle) 106

L

Lave and Wenger 36, 86, 132

M

manageability 50-51, 90, 150

marking 14, 29, 32-34, 38-42, 45, 86, 90-98, 100-104, 121, 144, 149-150

marking exercise 11-12, 22, 63-68, 70, 72-83

matrix 23-28, 33, 37, 40, 44

Merry 67, 76, 77, 81

Miller and Parlett 11, 13

mode of learning 88

moderation 38-40, 93-94

module assistant 141

motive, opportunity and means 114

N

norm-referenced 91, 94-96, 104, 150

O

one-handed clock 50-51

oral feedback 116-119, 121, 128, 140

Orsmond 67, 76-81

Oxford Brookes University 22, 29, 34, 38, 136, 145, 148

Oxford tutorial 27

P

peer assessment 10, 14, 20, 23, 39, 79, 90, 102, 140, 148

Peer Assisted Learning (PAL) 141

peer review 14, 22, 64, 67, 74-79, 81, 83, 85, 100-104, 140, 144, 149

Perry 15, 144

planning assessment 22, 45, 47, 49, 51, 53-59, 61, 85

portfolio 61

pre-assessment activity 22, 63-69, 71-77, 79, 81-85, 105, 149, 151

problem-based learning (PBL) 20-21

problems (with feedback) 11, 15, 20, 108-114, 125, 129

process versus product 113

programme approach 19, 83, 145

programme level 8, 19, 45-48, 56, 58, 137, 145

programme-level assessment 22, 45-48, 61-62, 87, 149

programme outcomes 46, 48-49, 55, 149

Q

quadrant 25-26, 28, 33, 37, 40

quality assurance 29, 48, 93, 100

R

relational dynamic 17-19, 21, 23, 148

S

self-assessment 34, 39, 64, 67-70, 73-79, 81-85, 90, 104, 117, 128, 140

Simon Williams Undergraduate Centre 138-139, 142

social constructivist 16, 24-26, 33-37, 40, 42, 44, 140

social constructivist model 24, 26, 33-35

staff cycle 39-40

Stobart 50-51

student cycle 39

student involvement 17, 134-135, 140

student satisfaction 12, 17, 135

summative assessment 9, 52-57, 88-89, 115

summative integrative project 59

T

tacit 16-17, 25-28, 33-37, 42, 44, 65-68, 75, 84, 86, 92, 97, 101, 109, 119, 133, 140

taking action (feedback) 112, 114, 119, 127-134

Taylor 103

technical assistant 142

telling 66

threshold 8-9, 11, 13, 21, 65, 99-100, 110, 147

traditional model 24-29, 42

V

visible criteria 72

W

Wenger 36, 43, 86, 132, 135

West 82

workshop 22, 34-35, 38-41, 63-64, 67-75, 99-103, 149

Glossary
(the language of assessment)

Summative assessment – assessment that essentially looks back and makes a 'snapshot' judgement at that point about the quality of the student's work and what it indicates about their knowledge, skills and abilities at that point in time. The focus is what has (and has not) been learnt.

Formative assessment – assessment that essentially fulfils a diagnostic role and looks forward to what the student might do differently in the future: weaknesses to be addressed (and how) and strengths that can be built on (and how).The focus is on future learning.

> **N.B.** Many university assessments attempt to combine both summative and formative, although there are claims in the literature (e.g. Butler 1987, 1988) that once assessment has a summative element it almost inevitably will fail to be seen as formative by the student.

Validity – the degree to which the assessment task truly does succeed in assessing what it is intended to assess (closely related to what Australian literature refers to as 'authenticity').

Reliability – a reliable assessment is essentially one where there is a very close degree of inter-marker reliability.

Module or Unit – the smallest coherent unit of study; the individual building blocks that combine together to make a course.

Course – an acceptable combination of modules or units.

Programme – one or more courses that combine to make the accredited qualification being studied.

Dualist epistemology – when a learner views truth in absolute terms of right and wrong, i.e. there can only be one truth or right answer; all other answers are wrong.

Relativist epistemology – when a learner recognises multiple, conflicting versions of 'truth', each of which represents a legitimate alternative, i.e. there can be more than one truth or right answer.